The Book of Business Plans and Proposals: Samples for Your Review

By

Michael Hedges

Copyright © 2014

Good Rain Publishing

Smyrna, GA

Front Cover by Mahceli D'Seghe

Table of Contents

Chapter I
The Business Proposal for a Product ...3

Chapter II
The Business Proposal for a Venue ...35

Chapter III
The Business Proposal-Plan Mix for a Product ...52

Chapter IV
The Grant Proposal ...66

Chapter V
The Service Proposal ...84

Chapter VI
The Non-Profit Business Plan ...92

Chapter VII
The Sponsorship Proposal...112

Chapter I: The Business Proposal for a Product

Prepared for Jane Smith

Prepared by Michael Hedges for The Sovereign Laptop Carrier

jsmith@gmail.com

(404)/555-2586

March 15, 2013

Executive Summary

The Sovereign Company, LLC manufacturers, markets, advertises, and sales laptop carriers. The product line possesses four models priced for a specific demographic. Within this demographic there is a diverse spectrum of consumers from students to businesspeople, to other professionals and entertainment consumer. The marketing strategy considers strengths, weaknesses, opportunities, and threats. The strengths are based in the need for laptop carriers and the fact that laptop sales have exceeded desktop sales for the last five years. The opportunity lies in appealing to a specific demographic who desire durability, yet seek style. Once the popularity of the Sovereign Laptop Carrier (RLC) product line expands, then a new facet in the market can be exposed and saturated with RLC products. Pricing is a particular subject that demands that the value be equated with the quality of product and the accessibility of product. Consumers are more likely to purchase a product no matter the price when its value, accessibility, and quality correlate with each other and the consumer recognizes that their core values are presented in every aspects of the sales and customer service experience. By aligning marketing, advertising, and promotion strategies effective means to gain new customers as well as retain previous ones becomes a clear path to growth and success. It is the superlative priority that a company maintain its integrity based on fulfilling customer satisfaction by aligning customers' expectations with their experiences.

Mission Statement

The Sovereign Company, LLC promises to provide quality laptop cases and carriers for the upscale consumer. Sovereign Company, LLC consumers range from college students to business executives to individuals in entertainment. The Sovereign Company, LLC ensures durable well-constructed products priced in the customer's favor for optimal savings. With the Sovereign Company, a purchase is not just a sale it is an investment.

Marketing Objectives:

- Augment the recognition and popularity of the Sovereign Laptop Carrier among the selected demographic by 10% every quarter or 40% per year.
- Present necessary information and updates for the target market concerning sales, added bonuses, new product developments and accessories, and the benefit of the RLC over competitive products to further augment sales by 10% per year.
- Overcome customer purchase objections by presenting information that would be available in consumer reports in more detail, utilizing customer service and proactive conflict resolution to ensure sales increases of 15% based on customer retention and new customer acquisition per year (Westwood, 2004, p. 3-28).

Consumer Market Segmentation

The overall demographic for the Sovereign Laptop Carrier is students and young professionals, age 18 to 35. These individuals seek a more "active" look in their computer accessories and a sense of individuality in style. The college students aspire to be or are young professionals in the IT industry, real estate, sales, marketing, advertising, entrepreneurships, and entertainment. The primary location for the RLC owners is anywhere throughout the developed world, specifically in the U.S., Canada, Europe, China, India, urban areas of western and southern Africa, India, Indonesia, and major urban areas of South America. Individuals who are considered white-collar professionals or students aspiring to be such professionals are the key marketing with the financial ability to attain the RLC. There is no specific socioeconomic market, however, it is more likely that middle and upper-class individuals will be more likely to choose and afford the Sovereign Laptop Carrier based on its construction and the amount of its retail price ("Identify Market Segments"; Westwood, 2004, p. 3-28).

Business Market Segmentation

The key segment that best serves the promotion and sale of the Sovereign Laptop Carrier is the customer type demographic of white-collar professionals and college students with technological fashion savvy who would utilize and desire such a product for its durability and construction concerning the transfer of their laptops. Such customers demand quality in laptop accessories. Many are always moving or in transition to one location or another and depend on structurally-sound merchandise to secure their laptops and notebooks. The constant damage of laptops and notebooks from drops falls, being crushed, hit, penetrated, or damage results from poor quality carriers; therefore, this particular demographic demands strong, accessible, easy to open and close laptop carriers that will protect their property as well as their livelihood ("Identify Market Segments").

Segmentation Variables Consumer and Business Markets

Currently potential RLC customers purchase laptop carriers from laptop manufacturers such as DELL, IBM, Compaq, eMachine, and MacIntosh. However, simply because a company can produce a laptop or computer does not mean they can design, test, and market a laptop carrier efficient to serve the customers core values and specific product needs. At the Sovereign

Company, specific strength index, heat resistant, and waterproofing tests are performed considering the most challenging scenarios to better design and develop laptop carrier that will not fall short of customer expectations and concerns which has resulted in loss in sales for the Sovereign Company, LLC competitors. With the rate of wear and tear on laptop carriers, many consumers find themselves spending twice as much on two competitors laptops in one year versus a Sovereign laptop Carrier with a warranty for the duration of two years. Consumers view the need for purchasing twice as much product as product design negligence and proverbial "double-dipping" into their financial reserves. Consumers seek products designed to generate the benefit of savings over time. Consumers seek products that are investments, specifically when they possess a lofty price. Consumers demand quality for their hard-earned dollar. It at this point, the Sovereign Company, LLC prevails ("Identify Market Segments").

Market and Consumer Research

In order to gain a competitive advantage over commercial rivals the need to collect and assess market intelligence is essential. This intelligence better shapes and defines the core values and product needs of the target market. The Sovereign Company, LLC meets all sales and marketing goals based on focus groups. Actually placing the product design via before it is placed on the market for consumers to interact with and observe is the best format to receive market research (via focus groups) and better serve Sovereign Laptop Carrier customers. Based on average retail prices, competitors such as HP, Vera Bradley, Targus, Incase, and Belkin offer similar carriers and cases for $40.00 to $120.00, depending on the accessories. The Sovereign Company, LLC offers comparable designs for laptop carriers and cases for $50 to $90. In other words, low-end carriers may appear to be more, yet the high-end carriers are far less which equate to more features and quality at a lower price. Consumers consider that a laptop's primary feature be durability and strength to support the weight of the laptop securely during travel. Next features such as pockets and sleeves with easy to operate clasps, zippers, and buttons. Following such features color is fairly important specifically for the key demographic which wants to look professional, yet have an element of originality in the work place. In addition, consumers respond to features such as heat resistant, waterproof material in times where spills may occur, inclement weather, or in extreme cases exposure to the sun or other heat sources can damage the hard drive and other features of the laptop due to poor carrier or case design("Identify Market Segments"; Westwood, 2004, p. 3-28).

     If a consumer keeps the Sovereign Laptop Carrier two years beyond the guarantee (two years), the carrier can be turned in for a $10% discount toward the next RLC purchase, including any particular sales campaign led by the retailer (i.e. Walmart, Kmart, Target, Sams, BJ's, Bestbuy, Staples, or OfficeMax). The Sovereign Company, LLC will offer a $10 rebate of the total of any RLC purchase for multiple carriers by one sole customer. Along with each RLC purchase, customers will receive a short referral form with their receipt. For any referrals that generate sales in conjunction with the original customer, he or she will receive a coupon via email for $10 off their next RLC purchase. When customers choose to purchase online versus at point-of purchase locations, they will receive a $15 discount on any RLC purchase of $70 or above.

SWOT Analysis

STRENGTHS	WEAKNESSES
The RemikoCompany is a new company with a fresh approach in consideration of customer needs in its product design	The Remiko Company is fairly new and not a well-known brand
Sales will be generated from the numerous opportunities for savings which will create a demand	Featured exposure via stronger promotion in a saturated market
The RLC product design based on construction, color, and durability are unmatched at the given retail price range	Product prices will satisfy customer needs, yet need to yield a significant profit for the company
OPPORTUNITIES	**THREATS**
Considering the challenged economy, the RLC price range satisies customer needs	Relatively new competitotrs that offer similar products and deals.
The opportunity for greater sales is based on generating popularity among the target market	Well-known competitors that reduce the overall retail price of laptop accessories
The number of deals, rebates, and savings opportunites appeal to consumers	Lack of or challenged marketing exposure

Market Position of the RLC

The best marketing strategy for the RLC is explicit comparison as a reference point with brands and their retail prices such as Laptop cases with the Aerovation Checkpoint-Friendly for $130, the BuiltNY Sleeve for $40, the Skooba Skins for $20, and the Targus Zip-Thru Corporate Traveler for $100. Aerovation promises that their laptop carriers are accessible and easy to operate. The RLC design is equal in construction and durability but at a far more reasonable price. For $10 less, the RLC design comparable to the Aerovation Checkpoint-Friendly sells for $90, savings of $40 off the Aerovation retail price. The BuiltNY Sleeve has a decent construction but for only $10 more, the RLC has a product line that is far more durable with key features consumers who use their laptops excessively. Similar in construction to the BuiltNY Sleeve the Skooba Skins is far more basic, and in comparison to the RLC, it does not meet consumer needs for key features that the RLC offers. The Targus Zip-Thru Corporate Trveler is comparable to the RLC, however the same model in the RLC product line sells for $30 less ("Identify Market Segments"; "Laptop Cases").

Marketing Strategy

The best marketing strategy for the RLC product line is via promotion to raise awareness in a more comprehensive fashion in which consumers are informed via numerous means in order for the brand to be considered comparable to current laptop case and carrier brands. From that point, the brand must exceed others in order to yield higher sales and to place the brand as a standard in the marketplace. Addressing the demographic of IT, business, and entertainment professionals along with students in related fields is the key. Considering the fact that the 18 to 35 year-old consumer desires to distinguish him or herself from others for a sense of originality is a key marketing point that the Sovereign Company, LLC utilizes via color, pattern, and texture variations, when competitors offer basic designs with less appeal to the eye and lesser appeal in price. In addition, durability, security, and easy access to laptops via operation is a consideration that the target market considers primary priorities. However, overall prices among competitors forces customers to either spend more or settle for less. The marketing point that must be exposed to attract consumers to the Sovereign brand is to "spend less to acquire more."

The Sovereign Laptop Carrier: Description and Features

The Sovereign Laptop Carrier (RLC) is perfect for the student or business person on the go. It is available in numerous colors and patterns among the primary, secondary, and tertiary colors, along with paisley and tartan patterns. The laptop is waterproof and heat resistant In addition to being a laptop carrier, it has numerous pockets for supplies, including pencils, pens, highlighters, and calculators. There is an accessory pocket for a drink carrier. The Sovereign Laptop Carrier is durable. It is constructed out of synthetic fabrics such as nylon and polyester with plastics and vinyl interwoven to given the laptop extreme durability. The product features one major zipper along three sides with a large pocket in from and a sliver pocket on the reverse side.

Once opened three pockets are revealed to hold needed school and or business supplies. Opposite the pockets, there are two straps to secure a laptop or notebook for easy and safe transportation. Under the carrier there are two "feet" set apart in order to set the laptop in the case on the ground for any temporary stops, securing the laptop for safety and protection. The carrier strap is made with reinforced nylon fibers with a strength index of 30 lbs, a weight far greater than the average laptop. The clasps and grounding connecting the straps to the carrier and all additional hardware such as zippers are made from a brass-aluminum alloy which is durable for years of transportation and the process of opening and closing the carrier.

Consumers are fickle and drawn to different brands based on the fact that the laptop case and carrier market is saturated with companies who manufacture and market computers and therefore consumers assume these companies accessories are equally efficient, or consumers are not as informed of the key features upon which sales choices can be made to benefit them. Consequently, consumers find themselves in a state of wasteful spending for necessities such as the RLC. Therefore, to build consumer confidence in the Sovereign Company, LLC brand, there must be accessible information on the product line via blogs, social network advertising, popular sporting and holiday events, point-of-purchase advertising at noted retailers and small businesses, print advertising in consumer-based magazines (i.e. Popular Science), billboards (near business districts only), broadcast advertising (both radio and television) from 7 A.M. to 10 A.M. and 3 P.M. to 7 P.M., and online markets including the use of search engine optimization. During peak marketing seasons such as the latter third to the fourth quarter (with notable dates from September when college starts to the Christmas season), sales campaigns with considerable strategies for savings, will be appealing and augment the interest of a growing market of consumers (Kurtz, MacKenzie, and Snow, 2010, p. 55). These consumers will range from buyers new to the RLC product line to former customers of Sovereign Company, LLC competitors. Due to the warranty, rebate, referral, and turn-in policies, there is virtually no objection that will not be met with a benefit in purchasing a Sovereign Laptop Carrier. The two-year warranty is reasonable, and with the addition of consumers being encouraged to keep the laptop carrier for four years in order to receive a discount on the next purchase via the turn-in policy ensures return customers and residual income. Rebates and referrals promote a more active sense of purchasing. If customers understand their role in the sales process goes beyond a purchase and directly affects the nature of the design, manufacturing, and marketing of the product line in relation to quantitative data concerning sales per model and qualitative data based on testimonials collected via social networking, the corporate network (sales concerns and customer service), consumer blog, consumers are more likely to purchase with the intent to buy again and share their delight in the RLC product line (Ferrell and Hartline, 2008, p. 29-58). There are four models in the RLC product line models available and their prices:

- The RLC Keeper for $50 features a sleek design, streamlined for transportation of a 15.4" laptop.

- The RLC Student for $70 features the accessory listed for the "Keeper", along with a large pocket for storage on the front and a sleeve on the reverse side.

- The RLC Professional for $80 features the accessories listed for the "Student" along with three internal pockets for related supplies (i.e. calculators, electronic devices, writing supplies).

- The RLC Specialist for $90 features the accessories listed for the "Professional", along with an external cup/thermos holder, reinforced waterproof lining along the inside, and can carry a 20" laptop such as the HP Pavilion HDX ("Hdx: the World's Largest Laptop?").

The initial sales campaign will begin in the second quarter of 2011, starting in April with orders currently being received at 70% of the retail price. Advertisement in conjunction with the marketing campaign will be boosted with greater frequency, specifically via broadcasting, to augment the anticipated number of units sold per month in the second quarter. The strategy is rooted in "Holiday Gifts for 2011". The anticipation will create more of emotional response among customers due to popularity and anticipation of the RLC. Although, the RLC will begin arriving in stores two quarters before the projected rise in sales per unit, the previous quarters will provide a great amount of data in order to make significant adjustments to better meet customer needs and product trends that are essential to expanding the RLC market. The projected peak of the sales will take place in the fourth quarter of 2011, during the Christmas shopping season based on the success of initial sales campaign (Stone and Desmond, 2007, p. 42).

The Organizational Strategy

Considering that the 4P's have been defined as the product, the Sovereign Laptop Carrier, the price, ranging from $50 to $90, the place, all major developed and developing nations (specifically within the business districts of their metropolitan areas), and the promotion, the initial sales campaign in the second quarter, 2011 (including further promotions via turn-ins, referrals, rebates, and online purchases) the product and target market strategies fit efficiently into the organizational strategy. Implementation of clear and concise data, both qualitative and quantitative via focus groups and other forms of market research and later sales data per quarter will provide necessary information to better market the RLC product line to the target market of college students and professionals. Through effective advertising that appeals to the target market's core values and consumer needs, the price will not be an issue. In addition, as the popularity of the RLC product line grows, then the price can be raised proportionately generating great profit via new customer acquisition and significant customer retention. Here lies the roots of establishing loyalty via popularity and recognition of the Sovereign Company, LLC brand (Ferrell and Hartline, 2008, p. 29-58; Stone and Desmond, 2007, p. 42, 197, 397).

Pricing Strategy and Channel Distribution

Penetration Pricing

The best pricing strategy to consider for the Sovereign Laptop Carrier (RLC) is penetration pricing versus skimming. Skimming would not be sensible with the RLC product line being relatively new within a market of established companies that manufacture, market, and distribute laptops or related accessories. Therefore, penetration pricing would serve the Sovereign Company, LLC more efficiently by generating a demand based on loyalty and low pricing for a given time. This strategy will bring a greater amount of revenue that will become incremental over a given number of quarters, versus attempting to create a sense of urgency and driving customers away with skimming, which would involve high prices that consumers may find unreasonable. This would push many toward considering competition and away from the Sovereign brand (Kurtz, MacKenzie, and Snow, 2010, p. 430-442).

As the RLC price would attract more consumers, a greater number of shareholders would buy into the company stock with the idea of greater returns in the future. Therefore, from a relatively lower price below market standards, the RLC product line would gain the momentum and popularity to generate revenue that would eventually surpass competitors' performance and result in a larger market share once the Sovereign brand become a dominant force in the market. The laptop carrier market is vast; however, many of the accessories in the design and marketing strategy of it go beyond the general view by manufacturers and retailers that see the laptop carrier as just a bag in which consumers tote around their laptop. The Sovereign Company, LLC will dominate the market based on design, accessories, and prices that are considerable in a time where there are more consumers in school than employed. There lies the target market in which penetration pricing serves superlatively. Consequently, as demand grows the prices can be raised with greater development in designs, thus further justifying the raising markup on the overall retail price per unit (Kurtz, MacKenzie, and Snow, 2010, p. 430-442).

Product Line Pricing

Product line pricing (PLP) is a key strategy that will enable the best sales results for the RLC product line. PLP is reasonable, ethical, and reinforces the sense of legality in a capitalist market. Fair competition is maintained with no slanderous marketing against competitors. PLP simply provides an array of products and relative prices for consumers to deem far more attractive, durable, and accessible than Sovereign brand competitors. PLP enables pricing that consumers will deem equitable considering the different features among the RLC Keeper, RLC Student, RLC , and RLC Specialist models. As stated in the RLC market Strategy, the four models in the RLC product line include:

- The RLC Keeper for $50 features a sleek design, streamlined for transportation of a 15.4" laptop.
- The RLC Student for $70 features the accessory listed for the "Keeper", along with a large pocket for storage on the front and a sleeve on the reverse side.
- The RLC Professional for $80 features the accessories listed for the "Student" along with three internal pockets for related supplies (i.e. calculators, electronic devices, writing supplies).
- The RLC Specialist for $90 features the accessories listed for the "Professional", along with an external cup/thermos holder, reinforced waterproof lining along the inside, and can carry a 20" laptop such as the HP Pavilion HDX ("Hdx: the World's Largest Laptop?").

Each model is priced in accordance to autonomous demographics within the target market. The RLC Keeper is perfect for consumers who merely go place to place for casual laptop use to say coffee houses or networking. The TLC Student is perfect for college students on the go who need additional pockets and fasteners for easy access to supplies. The RLC Professional was designed with the consideration that current professionals will use calculators, palm pilots, and I-Pads in conjunction with their laptop and will benefit from carrying all their electronic merchandise together versus separately, thus avoiding the possibility of losing items which can challenge overall professional efficiency. The RLC Specialist is much like the RLC Professional, yet with the number of windows and websites many professionals in the IT, business, marketing, and entertainment fields must surf between or display beside each other, laptop screens are growing larger. However, many laptop carriers have not, which can lead to drops and other damages to the laptop. Consequently, the RLC Specialist was designed to give professionals extra security in protecting their larger laptops while they travel. Maximizing profit is based in PLP of the entire RLC product line. By displaying the incremental pricing per product along with the differences per models, consumers are more willing to pay the higher price for more features versus for the basic model (Kurtz, MacKenzie, and Snow, 2010, p. 430-442). This will occur due to the concept of the consumer getting more for their money or the Sovereign brand slogan: "You will spend less to acquire more."

Value Pricing and Competing with Private Brands

Value pricing tactics must center on the concept of "pay equals performance" productivity. There are no legal or ethical conflicts, in utilizing this strategy. No consumers are mislead by any questionable marketing tactics. The company simply makes a profit based on consumer interest in the product line's value in comparison to overall prices and supposed benefits that competitors offer. However, their product line's fall short of a balanced correlation between product and price that the Sovereign brand offers. Value is a relative term; however, if customers do not see the value in the RLC product line design, colors, patterns, features, and accessories, then either certain models within the product line will not be recognized for the value or the entire line itself would be considered overpriced. This would result in a capital loss for the Sovereign Company. The company would have to consider liquidating the inventory for the current product line to gain some revenue. This cannot occur. Therefore, the value of the RLC product line must be seen as an overall benefit for the customer in comparison to the purchase of competitor products such as private brands like Foray, who design laptop carriers specifically attempting to corner the female market ("Laptop Bag Lineup"). However, with RLC models with color schemes, patterns, and textures that meet female consumer needs, a company such as Foray is far from a problem. There is the possibility of variable pricing depending on the quarter and traditional time of the year such as August is traditionally the "Back to School" season; laptops and related accessories are in demand. At that point, the Sovereign Company can sell the RLC product line at a slightly higher, $10 or so price with a rebate that provides $10 off the retail price; this will create a frenzy of savings, when in fact the price will still be profitable to the company (at the regular price yet below the competitors). Another strategy in value pricing would be, during the "Back to School" season and "Christmas" season, the Sovereign Company would offer family purchase plans with the purchase of one laptop permits the customer to purchase up to 3 additional laptops (of equal or lesser value) at 50% of the retail prices (Kurtz, MacKenzie, and Snow, 2010, p. 498-519).

Differential Pricing

Using the differential strategy is ethical. It does not take advantage of the technological challenges many face in rural America. It addresses the efforts by students and professionals to respectfully remain in such areas by choice yet address their technological needs in correlation with the Sovereign Company's need to make a reasonable profit. As far as utilizing differential pricing, it would be a strategy best utilized in areas where there was lesser or greater access to wi-fi or college and business district professionals. In other words, a RLC of any model would sell at the regular retail price ranging from $50 to $90 in metro Atlanta; however, in an area such as Broxton, Hazelhurst, Fitzgerald, GA, small towns in the southern part of the state, wireless accessibility is not as great and the demand is not as high for laptops or carriers. Therefore, for students and professionals in those areas with the limited market and likeliness that Wal-Mart, OfficeMax, and other retailers are not in the general area, this allows the Sovereign brand to experiment with sales prices according to the sales cycle and limited distribution outlets. When the demand is high during peak seasons the average retail price could be raised 25% above the price in larger metropolitan areas. However, when sales drop, notably in the first quarter of the year, the RLC product line price could be sold 10 to 15% lower than retail prices in larger metropolitan areas. Through differential pricing, the Sovereign Company would be able to create popularity in towns that large corporations overlook. Their loss will be the Sovereign brand's gain (Kurtz, MacKenzie, and Snow, 2010, p. 498-519).

Market Analysis: Size, Growth Rate, and Profitability

The market size for the laptop carrier industry is currently 13 major corporations that manufacture, market, and distribute laptops, PCs, and related accessories including laptops and 82 corporations from Axio to Zitteli, including the Sovereign company, LLC, that design, market, and distribute laptop carriers, cases, and backpacks. This is a total of 95 companies that are the composite of the laptop carrier and case industry. Currently, laptops themselves have outsold PCs. This trend began in 2005, and thus the laptop case and carrier market began to grow and profit. The growth rate to date of the laptop carrier based on sales of laptops has risen 18% worldwide since 2005 ("Laptop Bag Lineup"; "Laptop Growth"). According to the consistent level of market saturation, since laptops are far from a trend, the product life cycle of items such as the RLC product lines will continue for decades; however, there must be a considerable amount of energy in gathering both quantities and qualitative data to stay aware of market trends that define consumer needs and concerns. Through this strategy, the Sovereign brand can distinguish it itself and draw more consumers to its originality, yet remain profitable based on consumers core values when selected laptop accessories such as carriers and cases. Market profitability for laptops (including notebooks) has increased from 375 million units a year in 2010 to an estimated 75 million by 2012, an increase of 214%. Apple currently leads in laptops and accessories with 71% of the market that encompasses consumers with at least a bachelor's degree. The Sovereign Company must be able to duplicate and surpass this success based on the marketing template of Apple's success based in focused campaigns that expand on buyer power and supplier capability (Kurtz, MacKenzie, and Snow, 2010, p. 498-519; Shah and Dalal, 2009, p. 1-13).

Industry Cost Structure

The industry cost structure has to display a balance between to cost to manufacture each unit and the overall revenue generated on the wholesale or retail price in order to generate a significant profit. Currently, the estimated manufacturing cost ranges from $12 to $20 based on materials, assembly, and inspection. Sunk costs per unit are $5 to $9 on materials alone. Transaction costs are $7 per unit in shipping to wholesalers and retailers alike. Marginal costs are relatively low at $.005 ($5 increase for every thousand units produced). Fixed costs come to a total of $20,000/month per manufacturing and warehouse facility (in Marietta, GA, Lubbock, Texas, and Dayton, OH), $6,000 in utilities and waste management services, and an estimated $4.5 million in salaries and hourly wages. Variable costs may only occur according to time-sensitive situations such as material providers are not accessible so competition and secondary suppliers must be utilized at that time. The Sovereign Company will earn estimated revenue of $15 million in its first year. Considering the industry cost structure, marketing the RLC product line must adhere to the influence of competitors; no successful company ever feels as if it sells in a vacuum. Competing suppliers focus more on limiting information to shape customer perception and reception of their product lines than presenting clear and accessible product information. Incremental design changes are normal, yet the Sovereign Company must at times consider an abrupt design change or marketing approach that will challenge profitability, yet secure a large number of customers by satisfying their bargaining knowledge based on relative information that the Sovereign Company provides. The more consumers know the more interest and potential sales the Sovereign brand will have (Kurtz, MacKenzie, and Snow, 2010, p. 430-442, 498-519).

Marketing Distribution Channel Analysis

The current distribution channels are via online sales, retailers, telesales, and wholesalers. The flow of the RLC product line is best delivered through these means due to the choice of sales choices and behaviors consumers exhibit. The most direct distribution channel for the Sovereign brand is online sales at www.Sovereignbrand.webs.com. At the website consumers can surf from page to page and look at the vast number of choices throughout the inventory. Once they may their selection and place a payment with a major credit card of bank card with a credit card logo, the order is sent to sales department processed, then sent to the warehouse, then shipped to the consumer's home within a week. However, many consumers are skeptical of making online payments, even with guaranteed security from identity theft; others simply do not have access to credit cards or are unable to secure a bank account with bank cards of such nature. Therefore, retailers are the next in line (Rushton, Croucher, and Baker, 2008, 115-147).

Retailers such as Wal-Mart, OfficeMax, Office Depot, and Staples are key means to getting the RLC product line into the hands of consumers. However, the Sovereign Company does not have direct control over the prices that the retailers sell product. However, retailers can not sell product at extremes of high or low prices and cause companies to lose sales or lose revenue based on retailer actions. Consumers have more access to product at retailers; although, there is direct competition with other brands, unlike consumers who visit the online store and are completely focused on the Sovereign brand. However, the online store and retail points of purchase have proven to be exceptional means of distribution. If a potential consumer who needs a product from the RLC product line does not have internet access or a major retailer in their area, other than the few non-chain or franchise retailers the Sovereign Company may sell product through, there is the distribution means of telemarketing. Telemarketing generates sales far lower than internet due to its lack of popularity and the abuses many manufacturers and retailers have partaken in over the years. However, for the select group of consumers who do not have the distance or technology to access means to attain RLC products, telemarketing is available to establish sales and is a reasonable form of distribution. The Sovereign Company, LLC also is engaged in B2B marketing and distribution, specifically with wholesalers such as Gloneo Corporation, Ltd. and Linfair Enterprise Co., Ltd. located in Hong Kong. From wholesalers RLC products are distributed to IT, marketing, Management business, and even colleges that provide laptops for their staffs. However, the consumer is the primary means of revenue; therefore, distribution to serve their needs is the superlative (Rushton, Croucher, and Baker, 2008, 115-147).

Aligning Advertising Strategies with Marketing Objectives and

Goal

The key advertising strategies for advertising the Sovereign Laptop Carrier (RLC) product line are the use of broadcasting (radio and local/cable stations), newspapers in print and online, with the holidays there are a number of means to attract customers (i.e. online sales, rebates, referrals, and end of the year turn-ins, though they will not be available until Fall 2011), print media (such as posters and cinema slides) (McKinley, 2002, p. 93). Noting the relative size of the Sovereign company advertising will be a joint endeavor by the sales and marketing departments until profit and time permit for the development of an advertising department. The RLC product line will be promoted through Informative advertising versus persuasive or reminder advertising. Reminder advertising will not be a feasible strategy until two years of product profitability. Persuasive advertising seems costly, and with the amount of competitors who do attack each other's product, the Sovereign Company will stand out based on professionalism and humility. Both the brand and product line are new; therefore, the approach has to be familiar to the consumer (McKinley, 2002, p. 156, 173, 174). However, the products must be original and stand out among competitor products. Advertising will align with the marketing objectives and the marketing goal:

- Augment the recognition and popularity of the Sovereign Laptop Carrier among the selected demographic by 10% every quarter or 40% per year.

- Present necessary information and updates for the target market concerning sales, added bonuses, new product developments and accessories, and the benefit of the RLC over competitive products to further augment sales by 10% per year.

- Overcome customer purchase objections by presenting information that would be available in consumer reports in more detail, utilizing customer service and proactive conflict resolution to ensure sales increases of 15% based on customer retention and new customer acquisition per year (Westwood, 2004, p. 3-28).

- The marketing goal is to saturate the laptop carrier market with the RLC product line with four quality models between the prices of $50 to $90, resulting in high customer retention and new customer acquisition, thus expanding into other product lines based on the success of the Sovereign Laptop Carrier.

Measuring the Success of Advertising

Measuring the success of advertising will be based on observing changes in and trends within the market. Currently the trend among laptop carriers and cases is based on more accessibility and mobility, being able to open and close the carrier or cases, removal or placing the laptop within it, and mobility over a key duration of time. Therefore, there is great skill among laptop designers and manufacturers in using durable materials and hardware to withstand excessive repetitious use (i.e. vinyl-synthetic blends, buttons, and zippers). However, the future presents that as laptops continue to outsell desktops- a trend that has continued since 2005, consumers will demand more of their laptop carriers and cases, such as more pockets for accessories and cup carriers. In addition, materials will have to be more hazardous proof, such as waterproof and be made with safe, environmentally sound fire retardants. Currently, the leader in laptop carriers is Booq Boa Squeeze with a retail price of $97.02. However, its design possesses an excessive use of material. It looks more like a book bag than a laptop carrier. It is quite durable and has well-placed hardware, yet it appears to be more flash than function, when the average college student merely wants to be able to transport his or her laptop efficiently. However, unlike the Booq Boa Squeeze the RLC product line features a number of colors, patterns, and textures that are eye-catching coupled with efficient and durable designing that can be sold at a lower price (Kelley and Jugenheimer, 2006, p. 113-115; "Best 5 Laptop Cases").

Promotional Strategies Coupled with Advertising

The best means to utilize opportunities to shine among competition and influence the market in favor of the RLC product line is to stress lower prices for better quality merchandise, accessories per model, and the means in which to purchase product at lower rates. It is at that point that consumers will be more likely to turn aside from the numerous laptop carrier manufacturers and buy from one of the four models in the RLC product line. Advertising with major focus on rebates, turn-ins (after two years), purchasing online, and referrals (basically a gift card from RLC customers to a potential customer who will receive a discount as well as a $10 cash back to the original customer) (Petruzzelli, 2005, p. 48-50, 70-73).

Effective Advertising Strategies

Direct mail is costly; however, it is a reasonable means of advertising following another form of consumer data acquisition such as telemarketing or canvassing (a leaflet campaign). Direct mail would include a description of the RLC product line and have a number of coupons similar to those given with each purchase online or in stores. However, only actual purchases would result in "referrals" that could be given to potential customers from RLC customers. Telemarketing will be carried out by the sales department versus the marketing department in an attempt to produce sales versus the mere promotion or customer awareness. Based on the strategies that are successful in overcoming the proverbial "no" and other sales obstacles, the Sovereign company will have a better means to know their potential customer demographically and financially, thus enabling better marketing in key areas and times where and when such customers will respond. Email advertising is the most financially sound means to attract potential customers, yet there will be a need to distinguish the means of implementation from average spammers. Therefore, email advertising will be via data collected noting potential consumers most likely sites, such as gamers, online college and universities, social networks, youtube, and the Sovereign company website. Once advertising is associated with such sites by way of email or in conjunction with such sites customers will respond (Tybout and Calder, 2010, p. 315-317).

Door-to-door (DTD) leaflet campaigns can be initiated after primary data collection per customer demographic. DTD is a more effective way to further sift through potential customers for a stronger set of individuals more willing to purchase product, partake in market research, or share their experiences with friends and coworkers. Via radio and television broadcasts direct-response marketing coupled with advertising will allow for both promotion and sales to take place, simultaneously. This form of advertising and sales will be carried out between a committee of marketing and sales personnel. Marketing personnel will know how to shape advertising in such a fashion that will hold potential clients interest. Once customers call, sales representatives (unlike telemarketers who engage in cold or warm calls) will be able to upsale based on customer interest versus telemarketers who must provide introduction and presentation in order to secure interests with a potential sale (Tybout and Calder, 2010, p. 315-317).

Measuring Customer Satisfaction

The best means to measuring customer satisfaction with the RLC product line and customer service would be via surveys (quantitative data) and feedback responses (qualitative data). The survey would work on a scale from 4 (the highest) to 0 (the lowest). When it comes to a sale there are a number of factors that must be considered before the close of the sale. This is known as the customer experience. At the Sovereign Company, LLC the initial point of advertising, sales presentation, the purchase experience, and customer service will be assessed by the customer including their satisfaction with the product. The initial advertising will judged based the following questions: are the ads from Sovereign eye(ear)-catching? Do you recognize the Sovereign brand based on popularity? Is the Sovereign brand well-respected in your area? Sales presentation questions will be: How effective was the sales representative you spoke to whether they were a telemarketer or sales assistant? Did the sales representative listen to your needs? Do you feel that they assisted you to their fullest capability? The purchase experience questions: Are you satisfied with your product? Do you plan to purchase more Sovereign products based on the sales presentation and purchase experience (yes or no)? Will you tell friends and family of how wonderful your purchase experience was? When you call for assistance (i.e. concern, complaint, or feedback) are your questions answered to the fullest? Are the employees whether on the phone or in stores polite and displaying a positive attitude? Are employees informative? Product satisfaction will be addressed with a combination of scaled question and feedback response: How satisfied are you with the product you purchased? Please provide Feedback. From these questions, the company will be able to assess sales performance and the effectiveness of advertising. Evaluation will be gathered per quarter and addressed concerning revisions and or structural or strategic changes per fiscal year (Hayes, 2008, p. 83, 140, 158).

Gaps between Customer Expectations and Their Experiences

Gaps between customer expectations and their experiences will be addressed with proactive strategies that either reward or unfortunately challenge employees to perform accordingly or face disciplinary action. Disciplinary action related to poor performance is always a motivating factor, especially in hard economic times when no one wants their job stability threatened. However, with the number of potential and preferably retained shareholders that the Sovereign Company LLC will possess, job performance is everything. Poor job performance cannot be rewarded or tolerated. Initial retraining and counsel will be given. In addition if gaps exist on a great enough scale, then it is a matter of corporate restructuring versus individuals with problems that demand mere disciplinary action. However, when all proactive means have been considered and retraining has not yielded result within a period of a month, an employee will be placed on an action plan, then probation, then termination. For employees who provide customers with the best experience based on sales and customer service, rewards will be in order from bonuses, greater stock options, promotions, extended vacations, and other acts of appreciation. In addition, when key employees provide exemplary performance, their strategies and developments will be integrated into the greater customer service and sales programs throughout the Sovereign Company in order to provide greater success for the brand and better experiences for customers (Shaw and Ivens, 2002, p. 4-11).

Conclusion

The Sovereign Company, LLC provides a 4-model product line of quality laptops for general consumers. Economists have recognized a rising trend in the number of laptops purchased over desktops in the last five years. The Sovereign Company, LLC continuously develops and satisfies marketing objectives in accordance to the laptop accessory industry. As a new company, consumer market segmentation and business market sementation were the primary variables to consider concerning market and consumer research. The sWOT analysis indicates that the Sovereign Company, LLC would be in a lucrative market position in a rather saturated market based on the originality of the Sovereign Laptop Carrier (RLC) product line.

The marketing strategy is based on appealing to a diverse demographic of those who are laptop users that commute from location to location. These consumers seek durability and style. By providing such quality, customer retention will result far beyond mere sales. In other words the RLC product line will generate customer loyalty. Penetrating, product line, value, and differential pricing will be used to engage different consumers within the target markets based on their number of needs and interests. Penetrating pricing will be used to enter the market, using product line marketing to generate sales based on accessories that each of the four models provide. Value pricing is matter of taking consumer core values into consideration and translating them into customer value. At that point customers are less likely to focus on price because they will recognize the RLC product line's value in comparison to other private brands or well-known name brands that currently dominate the market. Differential pricing allows the Sovereign Company, LLC to attract a greater spectrum of consumers along regional and socioeconomic differences such as urban, suburban, and rural areas.

The market analysis considers the size and growth rate of the company, along with the profitability of the RLC product line as its popularity grows and its influence in the market expands. The industry costs will drop significantly as revenue grows per quarter and over time the prices per model can incrementally be raised. The market distribution channel analysis provides the means by which the product line will be presented to the public and how success will be assessed not solely on sales but how well consumers are served months to years following the initial sale. By utilizing customer loyalty as a better means to serve consumers not only will customer retention grow but acquisition of new customers.

The need to align advertising strategies with marketing objectives and the goal provides customers with better product and policy information, and better defines "who" the consumer is as far as needs and concerns for the every individual and entity within the sales process. The best way to scale success is to compare the numerous means of advertising against sales in order to discover the most successful form of advertisement. Promotional strategies coupled with effective advertising better illustrate the company's strategies to attract customer and serve them based on the cores they have when it comes to laptop accessories such as cases and carriers. When there are gaps between customer expectations and their actual experiences, customer satisfaction decreases and directly affects sales and the perception of brand integrity. Therefore, it is the priority of the company to delegate that all employees recall the mission statement, marketing strategies, value pricing, aligning promotions, advertising, and marketing, and to establish a better strategy in providing the consumer with the best sales experience and customer service as possible.

The Sovereign Company Competitors

The main competitors of the Sovereign Laptop Carrier (RLC) product line are the Booq Boa Squeeze, and Booq Boa Flow, STM Bags Scout Laptop Shoulder Bag, and Be.ez LAbesace Lime Drop. The Booq Boa Squeeze is the most successful, frequently purchased laptop carrier to date. The retail price is currently $97.02. The Booq Boa Squeeze is a laptop with a basic design made with quality material and features durable hardware. However, the design does seem a bit excessive as far as the amount of material. In some cases, it appears wasteful. This gives the carrier a book bag appearance. It in some ways can be cumbersome; yet, on long commutes it does appear to serve the purpose of protecting and securing consumers' laptops. There are a number of pockets with zippers, buttons, and hasps which secure accessory items that consumers may purchase in conjunction with their laptop (i.e. calculators, iPods, iPads, PSPs, etc.). In many ways, consumers are paying for more flash than function. The price seems to be more of a status symbol, than compensation for a quality product (Kelley and Jugenheimer, 2006, p. 113-115; "Best 5 Laptop Cases").

The Booq Boa Flow is similar to The RLC Professional with a sturdy design for medium to large-model laptop transportation. It is considered chic and durable on one hand, yet bulky with a somewhat '70s handbag appearance. The model is offered in a peculiar color combination of black and orange interior, with the odd coupling of an olive green or pearl colored exterior. From the medium size 4.5 lbs to extra-large 4.9 lbs model, the bag is considered heavy by itself with an even heavier price of $199, when the RLC Professional of notable comparison is $100 less. Here, consumers can see that price tags do not always indicate precision in meeting their ergonomic, commercial or financial needs. The Boa Flow is noted for holding its shape, a clear indicator that it will hold and protect the shape of the contents within it—the laptop and related accessories; yet, some consumers have referred to it as the weekend suitcase or luggage carrier.

Laptops from smallest to the XL do slide into accessible, steadfast, padded compartments with ease; however, the design seems more favorable for a wheeled carrier versus an armed carrier or case based solely on its size and weight. The additional three blocks of foam providing ventilation for the laptop are akin to gills on a large behemoth. Th e design does not have numerous pockets for certain accessories as consumers may anticipate such as a pocket for a smartphone, blackberry, droid, iPhone, or MP3 player. Although there are key areas that could serve as locales to place such gadgets, the probability of them being stolen, damaged, or broken are rather high ("Best 5 Laptop Cases").

The STM Scout is designed to carry Netbooks and MacBook models from 13 to 15 inches. It features a sturdy arm sling for the shoulder bag with a removable padded section. The primary market is for the consumer who owns smaller laptop models, which is not found in most product lines in the laptop case and carrier market. The laptop case is $49; a reasonable price, yet the product line is limited. Even in the colors themselves, the only few offered are gray, black, and dark green. Far from the scholastic look or boardroom appearance, many consumers have stated the STM Scout looks like a "man purse". The Be.ez LAbesace Lime Drop starts at $89; the product line is known more for its fashion than function. It was designed specifically for the MacBook or MacBook Pro. Consumers note that the product design is too streamlined and has the appearance of a futuristic aluminum case. However, the sturdy construction allows for high-energy commute. The models feature waterproof zippers, and a rather extreme design of a florescent, lime green or yellow interior ("Best 5 Laptop Cases").

Plan of Differentiation from the Closest Competitor

The RLC product line in comparison with the Booq Boa Squeeze and Flow is first and foremost priced far better. In these challenged economic times, Consumers are more wary with their wages; disposable income is low, so why should prices for laptop accessories such as a case or carrier be high? The RLC product line ranges from $50 to $90 for all four models versus $97.02 to $199 for the Booq Boa models. The size of the RLC product line is far more functional and logical according to the function and purpose of the product. There is no need to have a book bag or large hang bag appearance of the Booq Boa product line when carrying a laptop. It is true that both are constructed to protect laptops for external damage from hits to drops; however, there needs to be consideration of internal contents affecting each other with either damage or breakage. Here lies a design flaw corrected by the RLC product line which uses a limited amount of space to carry the laptop and accessories; therefore, producing the laptop from external and internal means of damage.

    Both product lines utilize well-placed and durable hardware. However, with the overall weight of the Booq Boa Flow with the number of zippers, clasps, and buttons makes for a clanking, cumbersome carrier. The design flaw with the Booq Boa Flow and the lack of significant compartments for calculators, iPods, iPads, PSPs, et cetera, is dangerous in that it could not only lead to breakage but invite theft. In no way, is the RLC product line invulnerable to theft, but what can happen is that it is less likely for any quick thefts to take place that could result in losses of such small accessories, due to the fact that the compartments for such items are placed both within and along the outside of the RLC Keeper, Student, and Professional models. The consumer has a choice of where to place his or her select items. The Booq Boa product line remains to be more flash than function. However, the RLC product line slogan holds true "You will spend less to acquire more ("Best 5 Laptop Cases: Booq Boa Squeeze").

The Sovereign Company, a Leader within the Industry

    The Sovereign Company will be a leader in the laptop carrier and case industry based on quality for a reasonable price, and the fact the RLC product line appeals to numerous consumer demographics that possess laptops. Within these demographics, from students to professionals, the Sovereign Company provides numerous opportunities for consumers to attain models from the RLC product line no matter their residential location, whether through key distributors (i.e. OfficeMax, Office Depot, Staples, and Wal-Mart) or online purchases at www.Sovereign brand.webs.com and delivery. The RLC product line is reasonably priced, far lower than the top competitors. In addition to durability and longevity, the RLC product line offers each of the four models in a diverse range of colors and patterns. ("Identify Market Segments"; Westwood, 2004, p. 3-28).

Macro-environmental Assessment Issues

The RLC product line takes into consideration that laptop carriers with a poor or challenged design do not distribute weight well and can cause back pain which has led to litigation of some brands. Although the laptop book bag is a plausible design, many consumers still demand the traditional laptop carrier design. Similar to Racel Zoe's Crossbody Laptop bag for $58.32, the RLC product line takes into consideration of back alignment, walking, and carrying the laptop over great distances or a duration of time. Based on specifications established by the American Osteopathic Association, the RLC product line is designed for comfort as well as function ("Rachel Zoe").

Capitalizing on the Top Laptop Carrier Trends

The major trend in the laptop carrier industry is to utilize designs that cater to the need for accessory accessibility, easy-to-operate hardware, and consistent commuting over a long duration of time. The Sovereign Company wants to continue to provide quality products to meet the needs of consumers, no matter the financial challenges (i.e. overhead, manufacturing and distribution costs). The key goal is to provide a laptop constructed with durable, vinyl-synthetic blends with buttons, clasps, and zippers that can withstand excessive use and at the same time be stylish for consumers from students to professionals. With the rise in laptop purchases above desktops since 2005, the trend for laptop carrier manufacturers will be better designs that incorporate hazard proof materials that are environmentally sound ("Laptop Cases"; "Laptop Bag Lineup").

Conclusion

Although there are a number of competitors that the Sovereign Company faces in leading in the market, the design, manufacturing, pricing, and distribution of the RLC product line is paramount. Many of the leading competitors have a significant consumer base, yet their pricing and rather wasteful use of material stresses flash over function, when the RLC product line blends fashion and form. The key to the RLC product line's appeal is to avoid being cumbersome and possessing a design that addresses the need to work with versus against mobility and back alignment, making the RLC design highly osteopathic. The number of pockets to safely and securely accessories and gadgets was specifically designed for the consumer on the go that continues to have a spectrum of activities and interests to consider while commuting from one locale to the other. The RLC product line is not status symbol worth purchasing, but rather a technological and economic necessity in which to invest.

REFERENCES

"A Chic Rachel Zoe Laptop Bag That Won't Hurt Your Back" (n.d.) CosmEpic Premium Health News <http://www.cosmepic.com/a-chic-rachel-zoe-laptop-bag-that-won%E2%80%99t- hurt-your-back/>

"Best 5 Laptop Cases: Booq Boa Squeeze" (2010) CNET Reviews <http://reviews.cnet.com/best-laptop-cases/>

Ferrell, O. and Hartline, M. (2008) Marketing Strategy. Thomson South-Western: Mason, OH, p. 29-58.

Hayes, B. (2008) Measuring Customer Satisfaction and Loyalty: Survey Design, Use, and Statistical Analysis Methods. Milwaukee, WI: Quality Press, p. 83, 140, 158.

"Hdx: the World's Largest Laptop?" (n.d.) (Retrieved 11-01-2010) <http://technabob.com/blog /2007 /05/11/ hp-pavilion-hdx-the-worlds-largest-laptop/ hp pavilion>

"Identify Market Segments" (n.d) KnowThis.com (Retrieved 11-2-2010) <http://www.knowthis.com/principles-of-marketing-tutorials/targeting-markets/stage-3segmentation-variables/>

Kelley, L. and Jugenheimer, D. (2006) Advertising Account Planning: a Practical Guide. Armonk, New York: M.E. Sharpe, Inc., p. 113-115.

Kurtz, D., MacKenzie, H., and Snow, K. (2010) Contemporary Marketing. Cenage Learning, Inc.: New York, NY p. 55, 430-442, 498-519

"Laptop Cases" (March 2009) Consumer Reports Magazine <http://www.consumerreports.org/cro/magazine-archive /march-2009/electronics-computers/laptop-cases/overview/laptop-cases-ov.htm>

"Laptop Growth, Soon Everyone Will Have Them" (2010) Articlesbase.com <http://www.articlesbase.com/hardware-articles/laptop-growth-soon-everyone-will-have- them-1591012.html>

"Laptop Bag Lineup" (2010) Squidoo.com <http://www.squidoo.com/laptopbaglineup>

McKinley, M. (2002) Marketing Alignment: Breakthrough Strategies for Growth and Profitability. Tuscon, AZ: Hats Off Books, p. 93 156, 173, 174.

Petruzzelli, B. (2005) Real-life Marketing and Promotion Strategies in College Libraries. Binghamton, NY: The Haworth Press, Inc. 48-50, 70-73.

Rushton, A, Croucher, P., and Baker, P. (2008) The Handbook of Logistics and Distribution   Management (3rd). Philadelphia, PA: Kogan Page Limited, p.115-147.

Shah, A.and Dalal, A. (April 13, 2009) "The Global Laptop Industry". The Georgia Institute of   Technology p. 1-13 <http://srl.gatech.edu/Members/ashah/laptop_ industry_ analysis_   aditya_ abhinav.pdf>

Shaw, C. and Ivens, J. (2002) Building Great Customer Experiences. New York, NY: Palgrave MacMillan, p. 4-11.

Stone, M. and Desmond, J. (2007) Fundamentals of Marketing. New York, NY: Routledge, p. 42, 197, 397.

Tybout, A. and Calder, B. (2010) Kellogg on Marketing. Hoboken, NJ: John Wiley & Sons, Inc., p. 315-317.

Westwood, J. (2004) The Marketing Plan: A Step-by-Step Guide. Sterling, VA: Kogan Page Limited, p. 3-28.

Chapter II: The Business Proposal for a Venue

Sophisticated Relaxation at Its Best

Prepared for John Doe

Prepared by Michael Hedges for The Club

jdoetpp@gmail.com

(404)/555-0147

March 15, 2013

Address, City, State Zip
Cell Number; Email

March 3, 2013

(Sponsor Name) (Address) (City), (State, Zip) (name of the person):

Imagine a place where you can eat, relax, enjoy music, dance, socialize, and generally mingle with the mature, "grown and sophisticated" crowd of Atlanta. This is the vision, the reality I foresee as The Club. The Club is a lounge I will own and operate in Atlanta which will blend the best of cuisine, culture, and camaraderie. For years, Atlanta has become a city of success in areas of industry and entertainment, but it has seen some of the greatest nightclubs and restaurant franchises come and go.

As a Memphis native, I was raised in a metropolitan culture rich in the history of commerce, communication, and collaboration. Memphis has roots is entertainment, cuisine, and trade as a city of crossroads spanning the South and Midwest. Considering the fact that the average individuals works two jobs these days to make ends meet throughout the US, I had a revelation to create a facility that would give people a sense of class and wonder, where they would enjoy themselves and reconnect with their inner celebrity by celebrating their hard work and in a sense escape the stresses of the work week

Sponsors, partners, and businesses will benefit from their investment in The Club via product placement, brand association, opportunities for celebrity endorsements, exposure to a cavalcade of consumers. When considering the draw of not only patrons, but companies seeking to expand their customer base solely on the name of The Club alone will be a lucrative opportunity for not only known but up and coming brands who can partner with each other and engender even more intricate and creative relationships between them

As a partner or investor, your investment of $10,000 to $25,000 will provide the capital to engender the commercial and cultural glory of the Club, adding to the overall economic prestige of Atlanta. In addition to an easily recognizable logo and location, the website featuring The Club will be a focal point of marketing, and promotion. With the website, a combination of brand marketing, specifically product marketing by association, personality marketing, and event marketing, The Club will mature into a profitable enterprise within two to five years.

Respectfully,

John Doe

Executive Summary

The Club is a nightclub that will provide the metro-Atlanta area with a variety of events and commercial opportunities. Atlanta is a city that has survived these harsh economic times. It is a city that embodies the concept of celebrating strengths over strife. In that sense, the metro-Atlanta area is a prosperous haven of hardworking and smart-working people who seek "good time". For a substantial fee, patrons will invest in their leisure and comfort for the ambience, interaction, entertainment, and cuisine that The Club has to offer.

Another aspect of The Club is the draw of the entertainment to the facility. There will be live bands playing a rich blend of cool and upbeat jazz, neo-soul, instrumental hip hop, R&B, dance hall, meringue, salsa, and Afro Cuban jazz. In addition, during key interludes there will be a DJ playing a number of songs to establish continuity. This will create an atmosphere allow people to relax and enjoy themselves with a sense of luxuriousness. Good music is synonymous with Atlanta, based on its rich history, its central location to crossroads in the southeast, and its success from the late 1980s until today.

The most effective marketing means to market The Club's blend of cuisine, ambiance, music, celebrity appearances, and noted events will primarily be through broadcasts, some street promotion, other related print media, and via other events in which The Club serves as an after party location or even an onscreen video/film location.

The Club will have no competition but itself, based on the fact that there is no other facility like it in the metro-Atlanta. Within two years it will be a city favorite. Within five years it will be a regional phenomenon with a diverse number of investors and partners stretching from New York, to Los Angeles, to Chicago, to Miami, and back to Atlanta. With the blend of culture, class, and culinary delight, The Club will remain a leading entertainment and leisure facility for all time.

Mission Statement

The Club is diligent in serving the needs of patrons and their guests as far as the urban, cosmopolitan nightlife experience. As the prestige of The Club matures, revenue will provide greater profit to reallocate into a budget that better serves augmenting the earnings of not only the Club but partners, investors, vendors and suppliers alike.

Customer service is top priority. The key to success is not just making money but having a patron-centered business. When patrons come first, profit will always follow. The more patrons, the greater the profit. It is a matter of reciprocity. By investing in the patron the patron in turn invests in the business. The Club will offer pristine necessities sought by patrons of the Atlanta night life, going above and beyond the norm that is now far lower in quality than the club/lounge experience of old.

As far as The Club's selection of food, health concerns such as nutritional value, dietary needs, weight management, and specific conditions that must be considered in order for clients of all backgrounds to enjoy must be observed.

The Club is dedicated to increasing the earning capability of all investors into the brand including, partners, suppliers, and vendors thereof. The Club is an entrepreneurial endeavor that caters to a vast diversity of patrons seeking the best urban nightlife experience.

Project Description

The Club will be an establishment where all patrons are treated to a sense of being famous. As they walk along the red carpet and through the grand double doors, patrons will feel a sense of being greeted, recognized, and celebrated. Patrons will feel as if they just walked into an Academy Award star-studded event. The staff will be well-trained and motivates to serve patrons and others accordingly.

The Club will have little to no true issues as far as establishing itself among the noted names of current nightclubs and lounges in the Metro Atlanta area. The Club's niche in the nightlife market will be easily established and maintained, based on the combination of activities and interests that The Club caters to and promotes.

Project Summary

Essentially, The Club is a lounge. However, this is a loose definition. It has a combined venue where cuisine meets live music, and live music meets the lure of celebrity. The Club is not simply a lunge, but a restaurant, a concert hall, and area for well-to-do receptions. It is an entrepreneurial endeavor with future possibilities to become a franchise in other major markets throughout the United States. The Club is sure to receive high marks and reviews in that it is not rooted in financial gain but the gain of loyal, well-pleased and entertained patrons.

The Club will provide an experience in nightlife that is luxuriant and sophisticated, catering to the fashionably and financially-adept. The Club will not be limited to the affluent, but it will address the needs of those who are happy to spend well earned income in a venue that provide them an experience that many never have the privilege to enjoy.

The Club will begin seeking a location just north of Atlanta in Fulton County sometime in April, and will open by July 2013. The Club plans to be the key haven for quality nightlife for the cosmopolitan urban experience. All parties who invest or partner with The Club benefit from the fact that not only will affluent locals utilize the facility, but international entities and individuals will eventually make The Club there home to relax and enjoy Atlanta.

Considering the number of vendors, partners and investors that will be working together on various events and projects in the metro-Atlanta area, there will be more than enough instances where business-to-business interaction will take place further bringing profit and prestige to all parties involved. This is an opportunity to ride a wave of success that is rising again in Atlanta.

Location

The Club will be located on North Ave. preferably on the 590 block in northwest Atlanta There are a number of attractions in the area and other key facilities for patrons' needs such as hotels and shopping malls. The area includes antique shops, limousine rental businesses, and art galleries. The area also incorporates colleges and universities such as the University of Phoenix, Oglethorpe University, and Emory University. The Perimeter Mall is just northeast of the area. In addition to being in a rather affluent area, The Club will be just south of the numerous international shops are areas of trade which is one of the most diverse areas in the country on Buford Highway.

Definition of the Market

Market Analysis

In a number of ways, analyzing the nightlife industry, specifically nightclubs and lounges can be difficult. There is an ebb and flow to gain in loss in the business. In addition it depends on the area or region such a business exists. Therefore comparative review is in order. The Club's primary competition for patrons lies among nightclubs and bars & grills, but no lounges equal to the draw of what the Club will be.

The Ultimate Bar & Grill, located in the Camp Creek area (near the Airport), is more of a comfortable food court facility that serves as a club certain times of the week. It has great food, and patrons are catered to, but comforts of plush décor and furniture are not available. The Ultimate Bar & Grill is a place for those who are eating on the go and headed to a nightclub, concert, or lounge. The Club incorporates all three elements of the nightclub, the lounge, and the occasional concert or celebrity appearance.

When considering the number of events taking place in Atlanta from videos by local artists, listening parties, and cd release parties, The Club will not only host these activities, but host film productions, conventions, seminars, and music celebrations and awards ceremonies such as the Hot 107.9 Birth Day Bash celebration.

Market Needs

The nightlife industry primarily in the nightclub and lounge market constantly is in a status of change, moving forward for the next big thing. Often the market does borrow from the past. In the Rolling 20s, nightclubs may have been segregated but all the money was green and there was a lot of it. By the time the 1990s had arrived, Atlanta had become a haven of culture and entertainment recognized throughout the southeast and later the nation. Considering, that Atlanta's Hartford-Jackson International Airport draws millions every year, the nightclub industry in Atlanta has an even greater opportunity to enjoy such prosperity.

Marketing and Sales Strategy

Market Penetration

Entry into the market will be feasible. Atlanta is hungry for a new venue that caters to the proverbial "Grown and Sexy", the affluent, 21-40 year-old man or woman seeking a venue that caters to urban tastes in music but cosmopolitan palates for cuisine. Contemporary artists, celebrities, and other influential personalities draw not only patrons, but partners, vendors, and investors. The Club's prestigious location will draw a diverse crowd who seek opulence with a sense of popular, but cultured flare. In addition, the number of hotels and other key businesses that will benefit from The Club, including the Hartsfield-Jackson Atlanta International Airport which could serve as a means to bring VIPs in and out of the area and over to the venue.

Market Strategy

The Club will strategically implement the common marketing channels. Facebook and Twitter will provide substantial advertising in addition to advertisements via broadcasts and promotional print media.

Target Market

The North Ave. area is northeast of Atlanta. It is in the middle of an affluent area which spreads into Fulton County, the international community inside the perimeter, and the Kaplan University, Georgia State University, Spellman College, Clark Atlanta University, and Morehouse College, and Georgia Tech area (primarily). This will provide our potential clientele access from any part of the metropolitan area, due to our central location.

- **Local Population** – the metropolitan population is composed of numerous cultures that seek a music and cuisine of contemporary Atlanta and the international experiences. They are willing to engage in new activities at The Club.
- **Tourism** – Atlanta has a long history dating back to the Civil War to the Civil Rights Movement to the rise of Coca-Cola, and successful music and movie industries. These factors attract a number of tourists who will make The Club part of their Atlanta tour experience.
- **Local businesses** – Due to our location, the traffic of commuters, residents, and tourists will prove lucrative whether these individuals, initially sought to come to us or were travelling for other business.

Project Risks

The risks are simple. There are established entertainment and hospitality facilities that provide challenges for The Club, if The Club were managed with a predictable, by-the-book corporate mentality or haphazardly like many who come into money but do not understand how to properly manage it. The Club will be managed financially with the needs of investors, partners, vendors, and suppliers in mind.

There is the risk that certain establishments will have a patent of sorts concerning certain dishes, music, and/or activity. However, The Club will serve all three needs and activities to generate greater customer retention without the backlash of appearing to be a jack of all trades and master of none.

More profit can be generated when The Club is treated as a staple part of the Atlanta nightlife experience. True, patrons will journey to other competitor facilities, but it is the all-incorporating originality of The Club that will keep patrons coming back. There is little risk as far as certain elements entering The Club not solely based on security, but based on the interests of the target market from ages 21 to 40, who affluent, and stylish, what has been referred to colloquially as Atlanta's "Grown and Sexy".

The first year can be anticipated as a year of learning via trial and error, but resulting in triumph. There should be a small amount of monies remaining after the start-up expenses have been paid and The Club is fully operational.

Financial Plan

Start-Up Expenses

Food Inventory	$4,000
Business Software	$1,500
Computers	$2,500
Signage	$2,000
Silverware and Glassware	$1,000

Seating and Tables	$7,500
Kitchen equipment	$10,000
Bar equipment	$20,000
Furniture and Décor	$40,000
Total Start-Up Costs	**$88,500**

Operating Costs

Fixed Costs per Month

Rent	$10,000
Labor	$50,000
Professional Staff	$9,000
Maintenance	$3,000
Advertising	$20,000
Utilities	$5,000

Total Fixed Costs

per year	$1.164 million

Miscellaneous Costs per Year

Artists, Celebrities, Personalities	$120,000

Variable Costs per Customer per Month

Food	$15.00

Restaurant Supplies	$ 5.00
Fruit Juice, Sodas	$3.25
Flavored Bottled Water	$2.00
Alcoholic Beverages	$5.00
Total Variable Cost per Customer	$15.25
Estimate number of customers per week	> 625
Total Variable Costs per Customer within 48 weeks	$1.83 million
Total Operating Costs	$3.114 million

Forecasted Revenue

Average Entry fee (between regular amount and VIP)	$65
Revenue per Meal and/or Drink	$80
Number of Weeks Open	48

The estimated number of customers per week based on 10,000 sq. ft. is the maximum of 1,250. For the sake of comfort, half the amount is expected. This is a total of 625 per week. Considering only a total of four weeks in which numbers are projected to be low due to weather or events external of the metro Atlanta area, there are 48 weeks with 625 patrons paying $65 to enter the lounge, purchasing an average of $80 worth of food and/or drink is a total earning of $4.35 million. The number of patrons is a general estimate for the sake of displaying strategic financial management.

Estimated Annual Revenue $4.35 million (not including memberships)

Estimated Annual Profit

    after Total Operating

        Costs $1.236 million

Action Plan

The Club will have a set schedule to serve its patrons with numerous activities that will take place on certain days. The amount of desired patrons per week is an estimated 925, 300 more than the projected amount in the financial plan. The schedule and revenue are as follows:

| Thursdays | Free until 12 AM | $20 cover and $ VIP | *200 people before 12 AM and 150 after | $4,500 in door sales, $5,000-$7,000 in bar sales. Valet services $10 for 2 and 420 | 30-50 cars $12,500 |

					for 3 or more	
Fridays	Free until 10 PM	$30 cover and $50 VIP	*250 people before 10 PM, 250 people after	$12,500 in door sales $7.500-$10,000 in food sales and $8,000-$12,000 in bar. Valet services $20 for 2 and $30 for 3 or more		50-15 cars $25,000
Saturdays	Free until 10 PM	$50 cover and $75 VIP	*250 people before 10 PM and 250 people after	$12,500 in door sales $7,500-$12,000 in food sales and $10,500-$14,000 in bar sales. Valet services $20 for 2 and $30 for 3 or more;		50-75 cars $30,000
Sundays	Free all	$20	*300-	$2,000 in		30-50

	day and night	VIP	400 people all day and night with 100 VIPs	door sales $6,000-$8,500 in food sales and $5,000-$7,500 in bar sales. Valet services $10 for 2 and $20 for 3 or more.	cars $30,000
Club Saturday Special Guest Performers	Free until 9 PM $60 cover	$80 VIP	*200 people before 9PM and 400 people after	$25,000 in door sales $10,000-$14,000 in food sales and $12,000-$15,000 in bar sales. Valet services $20 for 2 and $40 for 3 or more people.	75-100 cars $50,000

Membership Packages

In addition to loyal patrons, a select few will be chosen to engage in membership packages. There are three levels of membership packages will receive according to the amount they present at a given time:

Gold Membership ($1,500; only $200 members)

- 15% off food and drinks with bottle service included.
- Tables will be reserved as long as reservations are made 24 hours previous to attending.
- No waiting in lines to enter.
- 1.5% off any VIP section.

Platinum Membership ($2,500; only 100 members)

- 25% off food and drinks with bottle service included.
- Tables will be reserved as long as reservations are made 24 hours previous to attending.
- No waiting in lines to enter for +3 members.
- Complimentary champagne with a purchase of a VIP section.
- Receives personal invites to all special guest arrivals and related events.
- 15% off any VIP section.
- 5% off the Club VIP room.
-

Diamond Membership ($5,000; only 50 members)

- 35% off food and drinks with bottle service included.
- Tables will be reserved as long as reservations are made at least 1 hour previous to attending.
- No waiting in lines to enter for +7 members.
- Complimentary champagne with a purchase of a VIP section.

- Receives personal invites to all special guest arrivals and related events.
- 25% off any VIP section.
- 15% off the Club VIP room.
- Also have a special gift.

Future Endeavors

The Club will continue to thank the sponsors, partners, and vendors involved in success, in addition to providing them quality means of commercial exchange and influence. The Club will be Atlanta's most celebrated lounge within two to five years. It will be well-known throughout the region and cherished as an epicenter of fine dining, entertainment, and experiences that have long since been overdue in Atlanta. The Club will set the precedent for all other clubs that follow it. The greatest endeavor for the future of The Club is to be truly branded and establish sister venues in New York, Los Angles, Chicago, and Miami. Later, Clubs will be available in secondary markets in areas where the primary markets succeed.

Chapter III: The Business Proposal-Plan Mix for a Product

TWELVE/AM

It's a Lifestyle

Prepared for Bo Rand

Prepared by Michael Hedges for TWELVE/AM

12AMjoe@yahoo.com

(410)/555-1458

Address, City, State Zip
Cell Number; Email

December 20, 2012

(Sponsor Name) (Address) (City), (State, Zip) (name of the person):

Greetings, my name is Bo Rand. I am an owner/operator of TWELVE/AM. TWELVE/AM is the key alcoholic beverage that will set any scene night or day on the path to a good and gratifying time. Recently, I distributed promotional samples of TWELVE/AM among entertainment elite at the 2012 BET Music Awards. The response was phenomenal, leading to requests from potential investors for information on the spot. I have always had an innovative and aesthetic knack for style whether it has been in clothes, music, hair, or in TWELVE/AM's case- alcoholic beverages. As a distilled spirit, TWELVE/AM is destined to be a leading brand favored among a vast and lucrative target market.

Originally, I am from Baltimore. Baltimore is known for hardworking people who thrive through rough times. Whether people are dealing with rough, tough, or smooth ones, they all need a break from the grind. Nightclubs, lounges, and basic social gathering for the 21 and up crowd enjoys a drink to go along with a meal or while they are enjoying a song on the dance floor. It was in Baltimore where my entrepreneurial capabilities came into fruition. I began to experience numerous instances where I was around the right people at the right time. I learned how to conduct business by serving the client and reaping the rewarding of reaching out, studying, and interpreting the best means to serve the customer requirements in quality and supply to the fullest. Satisfying patrons' core values is the foundation upon which to build stable and successful profit.

I request an appreciated sponsorship and/or investment of $1,000 to $2,000 per month. I look forward to adding to your earnings and earning your business.

Respectfully,

Bo Rand

Executive Summary

Contained in this document, there is far more than a request for allocated funding as an investor or sponsor. Within this document, there is a detailed explanation of the product, prestige, and personality of the beverage TWELVE/AM. Through this contains of this proposal, TWELVE/AM is presented in a light that best addresses its ability to satiate the taste and need for fun and revelry by patrons and business owners alike. Without a passion for camaraderie and customer satisfaction, there is no business- no commercial success. Through collaborative financial, conceptual, and marketing concepts commercial, success between TWELVE/AM and its investors and sponsors is inevitable. TWELVE/AM as a brand embraces the philosophy of "Grown,

Sophisticated, and Stylish" everything else falls into place from that point. Considering, my personal growth and edification in the ways of brand management, strategic marketing that addresses the core values of consumers and aligns them with the interests of investors and sponsors beyond mere finances is the very essence of commercial success. TWELVE/AM is success.

General Mission Statement

TWELVE/AM's mission is to move from a local to regional to nationally-recognized branch cherished by patrons and businesses alike. The commitment TWELVE/AM will have to your company will be unmatched in efforts to continuously augment your profits and extend your influence deeper into consumer culture. With your sponsorship, TWELVE/AM will not only bring more customers into your commercial circle, but partners, investors, shareholders, related companies, suppliers, and media entities (i.e. celebrities). TWELVE/AM will enhance you overall network and the numerous events leading to greater accomplishments in the life of your company. This also includes not only raising awareness of your brand to potential clients but companies who will benefit from your commercial prowess and skillful means of increasing overall brand revenues through strategic management and powerful cross marketing campaigns. With your well-invested sponsorship or subsidy, TWELVE/AM will be an asset to your company's overall earning capability and earning capability.

Business Proposal

TWELVE/AM is a distilled spirit that will penetrate the market like no other beverage of its kind. It is not associated with any particular celebrity; therefore, initially, consumers do not have to "step-up" or feel the need to place themselves at some "Hollywood" status or related mentality simply to enjoy a drink that will always make them feel like a star. TWELVE/AM brings all people who want to party, celebrate, and enjoy life and the times connected to such activities together. True, as the brand grows it will be endorsed by the "who's who" of music, film, and other areas of entertainment, but it will remain as a distilled spirit for the people by the people. It will still have the ideology- the concept- of the local pub for local people- that hometown feeling where a man or woman can enjoy a drink with friends or stretch their legs and arms in a dance. TWELVE/AM is sexy; TWELVE/AM is sophistication; TWELVE/AM is success in a bottle.

Marketing Objectives and Goals

TWELVE/AM is dedicated to providing the most captivating and luxurious alcoholic drinking experience resulting in total pleasure and relaxation. TWELVE/AM's key demographic is 21 to 40 year old, urban male and female, social drinkers. Following a period from 2 to 5 years, considering all of the numerous combinations of commercial demands and marketing trends, TWELVE/AM will further diversify the selection of savory flavors available. By doing this, TWELVE/AM will expand its customer base resulting in greater customer retention and new customer acquisition, ensuring greater revenue and brand recognition beyond the hallmark of nightlife and the club scene. The marketing plan is as follows:

- Expand the TWELVE/AM's brand recognition among a larger customer base by 15% every quarter or 60% per year.
- Overcome target market purchase objections and/or concerns rooted in noting comparative brands via provision of more diverse-sensitive information.
- Distribute key information among the expanding demographics within the customer base to further incept the brand into everyday distilled beverage culture.
- Increase customer retention and new customer acquisition %7 per year.

Marketing Strategy

TWELVE/AM's original marketing strategy was based on point-of-purchase advertising and promotion at nightclubs and events. However, sales in this sense can be perceived as passive and solely based on consumers with a direct connection to distilled beverage drinking. TWELVE/AM will be more actively presented to the target market to induce greater demand among potential customers who may not be initially aware of the brand. TWELVE/AM will be known as more than a drink; it will be respected as a "lifestyle".

The Industry and Market Segmentation

Distilled drinks are no longer geared solely toward males age 21 to 45 specifically. It has become a diversified industry in which such beverages are custom designed and marketed to specific demographics that become hallmark target markets. The distilled beverage industry is far more competitive than ever; the reward is customer loyalty. Such loyalty is generated means of tapping into the core values honored by a particular market segmentation.

Market Analysis

The overall strategy for TWELVE/AM is based on a small S-Corporation structure with three to five executive administers and CEO and a president. The owner may be among this ruling administration would consider the counsel and influence of partners, patrons, and providers a like to establish the most ergonomics to distill, bottle store, transport, market, and advertise TWELVE/AM to grow the brand. Long after the initial promotion ends as far as penetration pricing, cross-marketing will not only ensure agreeable partnerships but establish customer loyalty among the very target market's initially held under TWELVE/AM's partners.

The Product and the People

TWELVE/AM as a brand has established itself as a smooth and regal alcoholic beverage that adds to individuals' party and celebration experience. TWELVE/AM is a beverage that will become a noted part of the celebratory tradition and experience. The people are hardworking Americans, who not only want the benefits of a great drink, but the memories associated with the "Great Times" and when they and their friends shared moments of happiness. In order to generate brand loyalty here, it is a matter of addressing the value of coming together and celebrating life that TWELVE/AM establish and maintain. TWELVE/AM was established in 2011; originally it was developed as a distilled drink for the urban, nightlife patrons in New England and the Mid Atlantic coast. TWELVE/AM has benefitted from lifestyle marketing, consideration of the consumers core values. TWELVE/AM has been custom-designed to address the needs such patrons have in a festive, alcoholic drink. TWELVE/AM implements exemplary brand management instruction in tune with new trends. This approach to penetrating the general market dictates the lifestyle branding that will ensure TWELVE/AM's success. TWELVE/AM will lead diversified and well-structured promotional campaigns that extend from cross-promotional activities to mass media events among retailers, partners, providers, sponsors, and investors alike. This will ensure means to generate interest and loyalty within each target markets.

Production and Distribution

Production of TWELVE/AM is based on regular distillation for the most part. Until a key amount of funds can be maintained, the production process will be based on mixing pre-made with the passion fruit mix, followed by bottling. Storage will be based in a general facility within a central location Atlanta, possibly near downtown or midtown, depending on pricing and availability. Within the two to five year period, following the moment of TWELVE/AM full debut in the Atlanta nightlife scene, eventually the distilled beverage will be carried in liquor vendors such as local and national "package stores" by the second quarter of 2015. Based on the marketing goal to expand the TWELVE/AM's brand recognition among a larger customer base by 15% every quarter or 60% per year, the industry cost structure will have to be adjusted, applying over 50% of the allocated budget to the new products in the product line by the first quarter of 2016 when the brand is nationally well-established. Considering the amount of anticipated revenue by that time, there will be no need to seek external funding to engage in product line expansion. Funding from investors and sponsors will be better allocated in expanding into market research, marketing, and advertising to further grow the brand and enhance partner brand recognition among TWELVE/AM's consumers.

Marketing Distribution Channel Analysis

Distribution channels will carried through direct sales to patrons via brand ambassadors at events (i.e. trade shows), wholesales to nightclubs and urban hairstyling establishments (i.e. barbershops and salons), and retail sales via franchise stores. Later distribution will be extended to online distributors. Sales will be fully monitored via data collection processes and assessment of related campaigns thereof to anticipate whether or not strategies are being implemented, effectively. In addition, specific overhead costs (i.e. gas) are substantially justified based on anticipated sales via such distribution channels.

Advertising

TWELVE/AM will not suffer the same downfall of many grassroots distilled drinks. TWELVE/AM will be promoted effectively with an ongoing, proficient marketing campaign. The advertising strategy will include social networking. Social networking has also become a better means to tap into each distinct "social" culture such as facebook, twitter, or instagram. With this in mind, TWELVE/AM, sponsors and investors who further promote the brand as popular, accessible, and beneficial with reap the rewards of the brands advertising campaign by association. A-list celebrities will be utilized.

Pricing

Pricing will not have any differentiation as far as wholesales other than the additional amount of revenue related to gas amounts needed to reach relatively far away locations. Retail prices will very due to the retailers themselves (i.e. urban and suburban establishments) and particular deals that can be offered to them based on bulk sales. As the brand's popularity and demand increases so shall the price. Value pricing is essential due to the saturation in the distilled drink industry and amount of financially-more secure and recognized brands whether historical or presented by celebrities (i.e. Sean Combs' Ciroc). The standard price for an empty 1 liter frosted bottle is $2. 800 ounces (6.25 gallons or 23.65 liters) of TWELVE/AM cost $200 to make 23 1-liter bottles. Together, the bottles and distilled beverage are $246 for 23 bottles. An average price for a VIP bottle is $150. The weekly goal of 23 1-liter bottles sold will cost a wholesaler $149 with earnings of $3,450 per week, and a profit of $3,301. Each bottle will cost will cost $6.47; each shot will average $2. Each bottle will earn a revenue of $22 (340% of the wholesale price).

Consumer Trends

According to Euromonitor.com, distilled spirits became far more popular in 2011 than beer. Overall sales in spirits surpassed beer. Beer sales fell by a total volume of 2009 to 2011 by 2%. In 2008, MillerCoors and Anheuser-Busch InBev merged and began an acquisition campaign to consolidate all of their holdings and assets. The merger was beneficial, but it did reveal that distilled spirits were gaining greater stability and growth in the alcoholic beverage industry. There was less fluctuation in the spirits earning capabilities. Overall pricing remain constant, and consumers were buying local spirits city and statewide proportionate to national sales. Here is where TWELVE/AM has penetrated a resurging market in the alcoholic beverage industry. TWELVE/AM is the new drink of choice by consumers based on tastes and shifting buying behavior of younger drinkers who would rather choose spirits over beer.

Competitive Landscape

TWELVE/AM is entering a larger market with the capability of growing into a company equal and later exceeding the accomplishments of Diageo North America in 2011. Diageo was the leading spirits company in the US, owning 21% of the total market. Its diverse portfolio includes Smirnoff vodka, José Cuervo tequila, and Captain Morgan rum. However, the company's influence has been influenced by the rise of new up and coming brands like Don Julio tequila, Matador tequila, Ciroc vodka, and Ketel One vodka. Therefore, this proves that with sponsorship and investment, TWELVE/AM will be a respected brand using similar brand management that benefitted Diageo as a competitor. The strategy behind marketing these brands has been through heavy advertising and promotions. This also encapsulates many of these products having foundations in history within the industry as trusted brands such as José Cuervo or celebrities who are household names like Sean Combs and Ciroc. Ciroc increase its sales volumes by 600% within three years of its debut in 2008. Therefore, with celebrity endorsement in some sense TWELVE/AM can grow substantially; however, similar to Ketel, TWELVE/AM can remain on an alternative path and still benefit as a selection outside of the normal marketing competition.

Prospects

The total volume sales of spirits are projected to register a Compound Annual Growth Rate of 2% within 5 years between 2011 and 2016. Consumer core values remain the same, but the demands diversify and change; therefore, manufacturers continue to be innovative in flavoring, packaging new product lines, and new strategies in acquiring numerous consumers who are turning away from beer. With age and socioeconomic-based marketing, TWELVE/AM will make best of the information and interests that consumers have to provide them with an enjoyable product. TWELVE/AM is on the road to impacting the industry.

In one particular by the National Restaurant Association (October 2012), 195 members of the United States Bartenders' Guild were surveyed and ask to rate the hottest 2013 trends among 123 items. A study 67% of bartenders said that the addition of culinary cocktails to drink menus enhances business. In addition, 26% stated that making culinary cocktails brings out the creativity in many professionals who often have to stick to a particular protocol of recipes and arrangements. 51% stated there has been an increase in the number of guests dining at the bar versus those who are dining in the traditional sense. 96% stated that the bar scene has increased in recent years and is more so an essential part of the dining experience.

In December 04, 2012, National Restaurant Association announced a list of foreseen trends in 2013 for distilled spirits. In "What's Hot in 2013 - Alcohol" survey of nearly 200 professional bartenders – members of the United States Bartenders' Guild (USBG), onsite barrel-aged drinks, food-liquor pairings, and culinary cocktails will be the most popular of drinks in club and restaurant venues. TWELVE/AM is a blend of these spirit categories, and thus is on the cutting edge of innovative means of pleasing patron palates and generating greater earnings for the brand, related sponsors, and much appreciated investors. The combination of more bar & grill combinations and lunges that provide food and drink alongside dancing have made drinks such as TWELVE/AM the most popular beverage in nightlife history. The top 10 drink menu trends for 2013 listed Micro-distilled/artisan liquors as #4 and locally sourced fruit/berries/produce-flavored spirits as #7. As far as the top 20 trends, organic cocktails came at #16 with signature cocktails coming in at #19. With this in mind, TWELVE/AM has a definite demand among patrons in 2013.

Estimated Monthly Costs and Explanation

- 23 1-liter frosted bottles: $46 ($2 each)
- 800 ounces of TWELVE/AM cost: $200
- Internet Commercials and Infomercials: $500
- Graphic Design: $400
- Labels: $400
- Utilities: $1,000
- Merchandise (hats, shirts, window stickers, other promotional print media): $500
- Email Blasts (Emailing bulk mail sent via marketing companies): $200
- Youtube, Facebook, Google, Yahoo, and Related Websites (SEO/SEM): $500
- Radio and TV Commercials, and Print Media: $700
- Distribution and Sales Travel (Rental Vehicle and Gas, Train, or Plane): $800
- Warehouse Facilities for merchandise, materials, distilling equipment, and product: $500
- Tradeshow Booth Rental (a one to two-day event): $400
- Total Needed per Month: $6,146 ($18,438 per quarter)

The 23 1-liter frosted bottles will cost $46 ($2 each). These bottles will feature the TWELVE/AM logo and logos of sponsors and partners. 800 ounces of TWELVE/AM will cost $200 to distill. Fruit and other food ingredients will be purchased from local grocers, specifically the Farmer's Market. Internet Commercials and Infomercials will cost $500. This portion of the campaign will begin within the first six months to a year, following the initial flow of sponsorships and investments. In the beginning the commercials will feature TWELVE/AM, the drink itself; later, more celebrities and/or recognized personalities will be paid to endorse TWELVE/AM via commercials on the internet, radio, and cable. Graphic design will cost $400. Graphic design will be featured on any form of media concerning TWELVE/AM and related brands of sponsors or partners. Labels will cost $400. The labels will be a smooth clear label that features logos on each bottle. Within the first six months to a year, merchandise (hats, shirts, window stickers, other promotional print media) will be provided for promotions and sales; it will also feature logos of sponsors and investors. The cost will be $500. Email blasts (emailing bulk mail sent via marketing companies) is $200. Commercials and other related broadcasts via Facebook, google, yahoo, and related websites (SEO/SEM) will cost $500. Radio and TV commercials, and print media will cost $700. Print media would be the last and least utilized form of advertisement and/or marketing. Radio is one of the easiest means to attract consumers to partake in the TWELVE/AM experience via direct sales or sales via clubs and other venues of festive, adult establishments.

Distribution and sales travel (rental vehicle and gas, train, or plane) will cost $800 for travel throughout the city and regionally. Eventually, national travel will take place within the first year after initial sponsorships and investments have been received. TWELVE/AM needs to be manufactured and stored, efficiently. Warehouse facilities for merchandise, materials, distilling equipment, and product will cost $500. An area of 30,000 to 50,000 sq. ft. will sufficient for this factor in maintaining the TWELVE/AM brand. For the occasional, tradeshow booth rentals one to two-day event, the average booth rental is $400. The total amount needed per month is $5,898 or $17,694 per quarter.

SWOT Analysis Summary

The strength that the TWELVE/AM brand will utilize most is being at forefront of the distilled spirits sales revolution. Trends always come in waves. In many fashions early Americans were crazy about whiskey and moonshine. Beer could take months to years to brew according to old German recipes (in most cases); however, moonshine and whiskey were distilled spirits of Irish stock and quicker to make. The modern wave has returned. Liquor provides a sense of revelry quicker and in some cases smoother than beer. The appeal is the strength. TWELVE/AM's weakness is that it is a new brand; thus it must surpass the initial point of penetrating the industry and being a respected name. The survival period of a brand is usually between 2 to 5 years before a business finds executive, operational, and commercial success. TWELVE/AM's opportunity lies in the fact that it is a locally-distilled spirit, and such beverages are en vogue. In many cuisines, there are recipes and dishes that demand alcoholic drinks to be served to enhance and bring out the flavor in food. With this in mind, TWELVE/AM will not solely be a festive drink for club goers but a drink with personality and prestige among the culinary elite. The only real threats to TWELVE/AM are other similar brands. Research into local and regional drinks of this nature must be researched in order for TWELVE/AM to better anticipate and exceed the marketing efforts of local and regional competitors in order to saturate the market and take over half of the market segment. By doing this, TWELVE/AM will establish true brand legitimacy and loyalty among consumers, partners, investors, and sponsors.

Sponsorship/Investment Amount Request

With your monthly sponsorship, ranging from $5,000 to $10,000, TWELVE/AM will provide significant opportunities for wide-scale exposure of your brand via product/services placement. Wide-scale exposure opportunities will be prevalent via internet marketing (commercials), trade shows, and press releases. In addition, your company's contact information and website will be listed at the end of commercials. Projected sales for TWELVE/AM are 22,080 bottles within the first year among 10 nightclubs, initially. When considering urban hairstyling establishments, tradeshows, restaurants, and entertainment-based events, sales will be substantially greater than forecasted. TWELVE/AM's target market consists of men and women, ages 21 to 40, urban and socioeconomically fit. These consumers are deeply-rooted in the nightlife culture. TWELVE/AM aspires to be one of the most successful and memorable distilled spirit brands of all time. Within two years, TWELVE/AM will be a noted and celebrated brand that will generate a wave of commerce within the distilled spirits industry.

References

"Consumer Trends: Top Menu Trends For 2013" (December 5, 2012) Food Manufacturing.com
http://www.foodmanufacturing.com/news/2012/12/consumer-trends-top-menu-trends-2013

"Country Report: Spirits in the US" (February 2012) Euromonitor International. http://www.euromonitor.com/spirits-in-the-us/report

"National Restaurant Association Research Shows Onsite Barrel-Aging, Food and Spirits
Pairings, and Culinary Cocktails as Top Drink Menu Trends for 2013 News Release. National Restaurant Association 2012" (2012) http://www.restaurant.org/pressroom/pressrelease/ ?id=2347

Chapter IV: The Grant Proposal

Fresh Start

A Music Program for At-Risk Teens

Prepared for Rob Hughes and Bob Wilkes

Prepared by Michael Hedges for Welcome the Industry Program

blahblah@gmail.com

(214)/555-4544

March 15, 2013

March 15, 2013

Hello County Juvenile Detention Center
2600 Lone Star Dr.
Hello, TX 75212

Dr. Do Right:

Within the music industry, over 80% of the headliners are entrepreneurial moguls. For instance, Sean "Jay-Z" Nobles (nee Carter), Russell Simmons, and Sean "P. Diddy" Combs are multi-millionaires. This is not solely because of their entertainment efforts but due to their creative marketing and commercial endeavors. Within the legal system, numerous foster children, once they become teens, are placed in the juvenile corrections system whether they are offenders or not. This is due to a shortage of resources to bring these teens and new families together. The Fresh Start program will be a non-profit, family-oriented, mentorship program in which coordinators within the music industry along with industry personalities will guide and instruct detention center youth. Tutorials will be organized music classes, rooted in arrangement, production, business structure and establishment, attaining DBAs, licenses, and publishing (i.e. via ASCAP), business proposals, attaining an agent, legal representation, and promotion. The focal point of the program is to give youths who strive to succeed and leave the legal system (or those who are merely displaced) a reward of knowledge and insight to own and operate within any aspect of the music business.

The program will open doors for a number of youth within the detained community. There are so few opportunities for children of all ages in Dallas, similar to most places in America. However, this program promises to expand young minds and expose them to a larger world of perspectives and professions beyond the expected, limited number of options for them to experience. Classes will be three days a week, established in a workshop fashion. The class size will be 10 to 15 students, considering the fact that there needs to be a significant amount of security for the teens and focus on them as students. To cut down on any form of distraction or disruption, the lower class size will allow for greater attention to be given to each student, whether they are in small groups or as individuals. Three classes will meet three days a week. The first day is a planning day (i.e. announcements of expectations and events for the week). The second day is an instructional day (reviewing homework, engaging in production/performance, and related assessments thereof). The third day is an event day (i.e. guest speakers or programs will held to entertain and further educate students).

Fresh Start is quite marketable as a non-profit program for affiliation by private sector businesses that want to partner or merely invest. Due to the overall annual budget, a continuous grant of $500,000 is a substantial amount to establish and maintain this program. It serves as a means of education, community relations, and will generate jobs as far as staff that serve the students, acting instructors, creative associates, and major label personalities.

When considering the future of these youth, we must think outside of the box. By thinking outside of conventional program formats which serve administrative protocols, we must cater to the needs and interests of the new generation in order to have a creative future through them.

Respectfully,

Rob Hughes and Bob Wilkes
Address,
City, State Zip
Cell Number; Email
Project Abstract

Fresh Start is a government-funded music program for youth who are currently detained in the Dallas County Juvenile Detention Center. The program involves classes, established and organized in a workshop fashion. There is a grave amount of youth who do not have families who are simply placed in the legal system and held in detention centers. They are placed alongside actual juvenile offenders. This creates a number of problems that can convert otherwise well-behaved but homeless/orphaned children into potential offenders. By the same token, the unnecessary detainment of such children adds to the overall population and creates a strain on resources, space, time, security, and opportunities for offenders to grow as responsible people and follow alternatives. Instead, many turn to a life of crime, loss, and restlessness. The life of being reckless ends when one feels they have a purpose, and that purpose once rooted in something leads one to creativity, loyalty, and progression.

Statement of Need

Fresh Start is progressive; it invites youth to think beyond the environment from which they came from or currently reside.

The Book of Business Plans and Proposals

Creativity is liberating, and learning the nature of the music business provides an avenue for youth to establish themselves as business owners and operators. These youth will be future leaders of proactive change versus followers of arrested development and wasted potential.

Fresh Start will provide the Dallas-Fort Worth area with a substantial amount of proactive insight and industry through the education of students within the legal system. In addition, to the fact that youth will receive such wisdom, opportunities to generate revenue for the state will arise from projects in entertainment related to music. These projects can include supporting causes to providing resources to local assignments and entities that are rooted in government-funded programs. For instance, music such as songs and instrumentals composed by the youth of the program will be utilized in commercials, documentaries, videos, programs, presentations, and events. Whether there is money paid to the city government for use of the music or not, money will be conserved which benefits budgeting, providing relief and in some cases creating a surplus, say monthly or quarterly. At times, in business, the money saved can make the difference in investments versus merely raising revenue. Money that is saved accrues interest whereas money made is met with initial taxes. Through this program and the fact music is an integral part of society, not only the Dallas-Fort Worth area will benefit, but the state of Texas will to the fullest. According to Econpost, Texas alone is the 14th largest economy in the world, ranking just under Russia.

Project Description

The Fresh Start program will be a program designed and continuously developed to serve the needs of legally detained and homeless/orphaned youth within the Dallas Juvenile Corrections System. This program will provide a sense of professional prestige and personal enlightenment in which children grow to be confident and establish stability on a path to an actual career in the number of aspects in the music industry.

Fresh Start will promote the concept of true change, strength over strife, and pulling oneself out of the system in order to rise above the limits of one's environment and the expectations of oneself. When students understand and experience being part of or rather taking action in their own future, they feel empowered and are more willing to invest time and energy into becoming independent and embracing interdependence. This interdependence these youth experience will be among equally gifted youth with focus on merit and accomplishment. The metro Dallas area is an epicenter of technology, commerce, and culture. Constant movement and mixing of activities, innovation, and ideologies have led the area to be a noted icon of influence and opulence throughout the nation and the world, but unfortunately, there is a grave amount of degradation that feeds into the stratification of the Dallas community. This spectrum between rich and poor is long and wide, but through education comes opportunity, and through opportunity comes benefits for all. Education is fueled by not only insight and training but money, and it is the financial support the city of Dallas and the state of Texas can provide to bring this original, ornate, and well-organized program from a mere plan to actual fruition.

Fresh Start will draw commerce into the community in the form of partnerships and sponsorships beyond government subsidies, providing greater funding to make the Dallas-Fort Worth area stronger economically. With such funding, more can be invested in public education, the infrastructure, and attracting more businesses to return to areas where many of the juvenile offenders and displaced individuals originally resided. In many ways, the program will generate a true sense of agreeable urban renewal by incorporating, versus excluding, the needs and thoughts of the existing communities in these socioeconomically-challenged areas.

Youth will seek to be involved in the program, and with greater recruitment there would be greater funding due to the demand and further information of the program. More money means more opportunities to extend the program into transitional housing facilities (halfway houses) and to better provide tiers of sociological, cognitive, and psycho-emotional development for program attendees. The Fresh Start program, serving as a liaison, will follow the attendees from the detention center, to transitional housing facilities, and then back into schools, and even into college. Many times, programs designed to assist such individuals and better their lives fall to the wayside due to disuse or lesser focus. This disuse is rooted in incomplete implementation. Often times, youth are made to feel that they are cared for and supported, but when programs end with no outlets to related activities or associations, such youth often feel abandoned and delve deeper into the most non-conducive or precarious situations.

Within five to ten years, Fresh Start will be a fully-funded government program. It will not be limited to Texas but will exist throughout all of the major metropolitan areas in the nation. These areas that are primarily populated by the highest juvenile offender populations such as Dallas-Fort Worth, Houston, Atlanta, Miami, New York City, Cleveland, Detroit, Cincinnati, Chicago, St. Louis, Los Angeles, Baltimore, Washington, D.C., and the San Francisco (Bay Area).

Goals and Objectives

Diligently, Fresh Start will strive and continue to develop into a program that enables youth to step out of their current dilemmas, whether they are rooted in crime, homelessness, or having an orphan status. When youth are educated and take interest in the actual information they are receiving for the application of skills and talent in their own community, they are more apt to remain on a path of continuous achievement and proficiency. In other words, they think "succeeding is cool!" There is a certain popularity that all people adore and honor when it comes to successful people. In many cases, there are numerous negative or absent role models in youths' lives, but Fresh Start will not only provide celebrity mentors and guest speakers, but regular, everyday people, men and women, who are from the same communities as these youth. These instructors and mentors will show them that they can make it, and they will succeed.

The objectives of the Fresh Start program outline the purpose and perspectives that have and will continue to shape the path upon which youth will be prepared to enter and/or reenter society as skillful and socially well-adapted members of society with well-grounded dreams of attaining careers in the music industry.

The main operational objectives include:

- To provide an educational program in which students learn the numerous aspects of the music industry.
- To learn basic recording and production (technology).
- To understand arrangement and project management (human resources).
- To be aware of licensing and publishing practices (business management).
- To respect all general racial, religious, or gender differences (i.e. Equal Employment Opportunity adherence and compliance and the legal system).
- To be socially adept and professionally proficient (cognitive education, behavior modification, conflict resolution, and communication skills).
- To better understand and utilize constructive criticism in order to revise and redevelop cognitive and technical abilities in order to succeed.
- To continuously develop the mentorship of Fresh Start.
- To support instructors, mentors, and staff financially, ethically, and socially.
- To promote overall congruence throughout the program among all individuals.

The main executive objectives include:

- Engendering a workforce within the juvenile offender population that once released will return to school and the home or housing facility (under parental or custodial care) with the intention of entering the workforce, post-secondary program, or military.
- Continuously developing the combination of education and entertainment with a focus on productivity and progress of reconstructing and establishing stronger urban communities.
- Enabling socioeconomically-challenged students to hone skills that they can use to generate money ethically and invest such income responsibly, whether they join the corporate workforce or take on entrepreneurial endeavors.
- Expand the Fresh Start program around the state of Texas, then throughout the southwestern United States, and later around the nation in key metropolitan areas that would best benefit from this program.
- To reduce schedule conflicts, collateral damages, overlapping redundancy in policy or practice throughout the program.

The main financial objectives include:

- To sufficiently reallocate all federal, state, and local subsidies, charitable donations, and revenues generated through commercial projects to the Fresh Start budget annually.
- To develop and maintain a committee that words with the Board of Directors, Chairman, and or President of Fresh Start to report, advise, and present means of quality fiscal spending via functional systems thinking, plausible accounting practices, or strategic investments.
- To seek new lucrative partnerships, fellowships, and philanthropic endeavors to further the financial agenda of Fresh Start to grow and mature into a national program

with affiliation in numerous industries in order to augment funding youth and communities benefitting from the program.

The goals of the Fresh Start program outline the results that will continue to be expected as far as enabling the betterment of youth who are within the juvenile legal system to prosper and discovery liberation and stability through education and entertainment in the world of music. As these goals are accomplished, the youth will not solely be students, but become educators and mentors in their own right, whether they remain affiliated with Fresh Start or go out into other career or community pursuits.

The main operational goals include:

- Students will engage in a four-year program from ages 6 to 18 years-old. This is due to the fact that not all students will enter the detention facility, be released from it, or be adopted at the same time. Each year they will engage in a self-contained curriculum that integrates public school standard education with technical training in music recording equipment, and industry-related brand management, and extensive knowledge in generally business and social etiquette.
- 45 Students will meet in 3 classes 3 days a week. There will be 15 students in each class. The first day is a planning day (i.e. announcements of expectations and events for the week). The second day is an instructional day (reviewing homework, engaging in production/performance, and related assessments thereof). The third day is an event day (i.e. guest speakers or programs will held to entertain and further educate students). Each class is 90 minutes unless specified otherwise.
- Students will be aware and able to record, mix, and later master at least one 3-minute song within a group of four

The Book of Business Plans and Proposals 75

youths per year with significant professional assessment and the opportunity to submit the project to actual music industry professionals.
- Students will skillfully be able to organize concept meetings, practices, recording sessions, arrangements, mixing, mastering, and listening (assessment) sessions.
- Students will be aware and capable of attaining licenses as professional musicians and engage publishing practices within organizations such as SESAC, ASCAP, and BMI. Students will have knowledge of IRSC (International Standard Recording Code) numbers, authentic barcoding, and knowledge of the Big Four (major labels: Sony BMG, Universal Music Group, EMI, Warner Music Group) .
- Students will respect and be aware of laws that protect the rights of all people against harassment or any form of discrimination.
- Students will be well-behaved and proficiently competent with a focus in the music industry alongside proactive outlooks and skills concerning academic subject matters.
- Many students will seek to remain in the Fresh Start program, pursue post-secondary degrees, and military careers (if they are of such an age).
- Students will receive a certificate of completion once they have completed the four years in the program. This will make them far more attractive to potential adoptive parents and/or educational/occupational programs.
- All staff and instructional parties involved will feel a sense of accomplishment and partake in students' achievements.

The main executive goals include:

- The juvenile offender/displaced population will become able-bodied, competent individuals who will mature and pursue a stable career in either the music industry or related industries involving that once released will return to school and the home or housing facility (under parental or

custodial care) with the intention of entering the workforce, post-secondary program, or military (if they are of such age).
- Urban communities that were or remain the residence of former juvenile offenders will socioeconomically improve and become financially functional based on the proactive influence of the Fresh Start Program and reputable skills provided by the students.
- Students will enter the workforce with ease in careers in corporate America at middle management to executive level.
- The Fresh Start program will be grow from a local program to a state program, to a regional, and later a national program to engender educational advancement, socially adeptness, and professional career-based capabilities.
- Through skillful and concise management conflicts, losses, and damages will be significantly reduced if not mitigated completely.

The main financial goals include:

- The Board of Directors, Chairman, and/or President of Fresh Start will report, advise, and present means of strategic investment of all subsidies, donations, and revenues. The plan is to then review and place all revenues back into the budget the following year. This will serve as a financial foundation to further build and expand the Fresh Start program into a national program.

Budget

The budget for Fresh Start will be established alongside the frequency of subsidies and donations received per year according to Dallas-Fort Worth and the state of Texas' fiscal schedules and practices. The budget will be aligned per project or development with the general fiscal schedules to maximize the allocation of funding per quarter and per year in order to provide the best financial support and investment for the youth. All expenses such as fixed and variable costs are included.

Fresh Start will be a budgeted based on resource and funding accessibility versus mere availability. Simply having money available to be afforded with no clear path as to the accessibility to invest it in projects and practices with considerable time management is wasteful. Therefore, Fresh Start will be organized with systems thinking that is founded deeper in forecasted revenues for reallocation versus merely the amount of profit that can be made per year. The reciprocity between funding earned/received and the finances that remain that can be invested will ensure that considerable savings practices enable growth through exponential financial procedures versus seemingly random, loose, or casual spending that many organizations and programs undergo. In other words, strategic investment and reallocation of funding will enable Fresh Start to thrive versus merely survive. Spending is myopic without consideration of consistent, well-planned reinvestment of revenue to generate a healthy budget for the following fiscal year.

Budget	Item	Quantity	Total
Facility and Utilities	Large Classroom (Writing Lab, Recording Lab, Group Study, Lecture/Seminar Room)	1 (est. 1000 sq. ft)	$2,500 for the facility; the actual electricity will demand an additional $20,000 to the original electric bill for the entire detention center facility.

Training	Instructors	7 (6 regular; 1 floater)	$210,000
Books	Production, Management, and Business Etiquette Textbooks	Up to 3 per student. With 45 students that is 135. $400 per book.	$54,000
Computers	Macs (Recording) and PC (Word processing) Pro Tools	15 of both. A total of 30 Pro tool Installation for the Macs only	$1,300 per Mac; $900 per PC. For the "pair",15 each is a total of $33,000 $ 15,000
Production Equipment (i.e. Recording, Mixing, Mastering)	Hardware, Soundboards, Microphones, Monitors, Mixers, Software, Booth Materials, Accessories	Varies. Requires upkeep…	$25,000
Guest Speakers	Celebrities, Industry Personalities, Community Leaders	2 speakers per month: 1 industry leader, 1 community leader.	$5,000 per industry leader; $1,000 per community leader. $6,000 per month; $72,000 per year
Total			$431,500

Facility

The facility will actually be a 1000 sq. ft area within one of the larger areas at the Dallas juvenile correctional facility. Within this space, there would be an area prepared for a computer lab with both Macs and PCs and an ample space for students to work and interact. A second area in the room would be specified for a general classroom. In this area, discussions, lessons, and seminars would take place as well as receiving speakers, even for small luncheons and celebrations. A third area will be set off to the side for a studio. Within this studio, there will be a basic recording booth, an open area for instrument playing, and a smaller area serving as a sound room for vocals. The three major areas will be designated as the Writing Lab, the Classroom, and the Recording Lab. Although, there is no direct rent paid to the detention center, the fact that the space could be used for other activities in essence costs money. In order to maintain the entire facility for Fresh Start, the cost will be $2,500 per year. The actual electricity will demand an additional $20,000 to the original electric bill for the entire detention center facility. This is due to the amount used to power computers, studio equipment, lighting, and HVAC.

Training

Training will be carried out by instructors and mentors. Instructors and mentors will be selected from numerous, reputable colleges and universities with degrees in education, business, sociology, and psychology. As stated earlier, instructors and mentors will engage in three 90- minute classes per week with students. The areas of focus will be education comparable to high school classes, business and entertainment management courses, and sound recording courses with a focus on collaboration and interdependence. There will be three instructors and four mentors.

One mentor will float from class to class throughout the week when needed. Instructors will engage in basic lecture, small group, and large group activities and presentation. All mentors and instructors will be K-12 certified. Homework will be assigned; tests and other assessments will be given alongside key music industry projects. All instruction will be comparable to the Dallas County Independent School District. The total amount for seven educational employees at $30,000 is $210,000.

Books

The text books needed will be well-written instructional literature with focuses in general education, business management, and sound recording. The general education will cover language arts (American and British literature and general grammar). The business management books will provide the general template for strategic planning, systems thinking, implementation, and understanding of basic terms and functions of entry-level and mid-level management along with upper administrative management. There will be key lessons in the roles of presidents, chairpersons, the board of directors, CEOs, CFOs, and COOs. There will be key lessons on marketing as far as target markets, core values, product lines, branding, advertisement, and promotion. In addition, a text will be provided that covers the numerous areas of entertainment law as far as adherence and compliance to copyrights and avoiding infringement, basic deals, publishing, song writing, managing, promotion, artists, and choreography. As far as the technical texts, subjects such as hardware and software and means to construct, maintain, and upgrade sound studios will be covered, along with cinematography, lighting, establishing mise-en-scene, and audio/visual skills such as aligning images and sound for film or video. Each book will be about $400. For 45 students with 3 books each, the total is $54,000.

Computers

The computers that will be bought are Macs and PCs. The Macs are perfect for recording. They have numerous features as far as quicker processors capable of generating standard-level audio/visual production. In addition, software such as Pro Tools (an additional $1,000 per computer) will be installed on each Mac. The PCs are best for word processing, specifically due to Windows and the ease at which to navigate when typing, handling graphics (also available on Mac), and generating charts. Students will primarily maintain emails, writing assignments, any social media strictly used for maintaining their music pages on the PC (i.e. emails and websites) will be strictly monitored. Certain search engines will be blocked. The Macs are an average of $1,300 each; the PCs are an average of $900 each. A total of $33,000 will be paid each year for 15 "pairs" of computers.

Production Equipment

Production equipment will range from hardware, soundboards, microphones, monitors, mixers, software, booth materials, to accessories (i.e. headphones, patch cords, microphone covers, acoustic gear, music instruments, and related materials). For the most part, the sound board and display has to be accurate in order for students to understand the need for precision in recording and overall production. A number of compressors for effects such as reverb, flarangers, and synthesizer effects are necessary to understand for basic song production. Students will understand elements of vibro-acoustics (the psychics of sound), placement of microphones and monitors, even for live performance, and other key elements of music production that brings out the beat out or recording or performance. Key brands that will be purchased are Nuemann, Yamaha, Kurzwei, Telefunken. The overall price for maintenance and new material acquisition will be $25,000 annually.

Guest Speakers

Guest speakers will include a number of the contemporary producers and artists that are popular to the youth, yet have a proactive message or foundation in community. The key artists will be from Arista, Epic, Island Def Jam, EMI brands, and others. In addition there will be local artists from Stampede Records and other well-known Dallas labels. There will be speakers from the community who are involved in furthering youths' education, their journey into the military and/or religious leadership. In addition, there will be leaders in legal and business-related fields who will speak to the students concerning their future in business, socialization, even family planning. The overall price for speakers will be $72,000 per year.

Summary

When it comes to the future of numerous displaced youth and juvenile offenders, the detention center experience can negatively affect them, creating criminals who otherwise would not exist if they had an opportunity as youth to head in a healthy direction. Fresh Start is a government-funded music program that will satisfy this need. This program combines general education, technical knowhow of recording, and wisdom rooted in the music business and entertainment law. The purpose of the program is to provide a sense of community and family among instructors, mentors, speakers, and others who provide guidance and focus for the youth. The purpose of Fresh Start is to assist youth in embracing their creativity, discovering their intellect, and developing their talents. Through creativity, youth can be liberated and mature into productive citizens. With the subsidies, donations, and other sources of funding, revenues will be raised and reallocated, expanding the capabilities of the program. Later, the success in Dallas will lead to the Fresh Start program existing in numerous detentions centers across the country which will assist in the improvement of the upcoming generation.

Chapter V: The Service Proposal

Lavish Wash Will Provide APS the Best Bus Cleaning Service

The Lavish Bus Wash Endeavor

Prepared for All-City Public Schools

Prepared by Michael Hedges for Brown Investment Group (DBA Lavish Wash)

3485 N. Hill St.SE
Smyrna, Georgia 30080
(770) 555-0786
info@lavishwashAll-City.com
July 27, 2011

Statement of Confidentiality & Non-disclosure

This document encloses proprietary and confidential, commercial and financial information. All data provided to All-City Public Schools is submitted upon its agreement not to disclose such information contained thereof except in the context and legal parameters of commercial endeavors with Brown Investment Group (DBA Lavish Wash) The recipient of this document consents to notify current and potential employees of Brown Investment Group (DBA Lavish Wash) who possess access to detailed and sensitive content as confidential.

The recipient establishes agreement to instruct each employee that disclosure of the content within these documents is forbidden, unless with a member who is working directly with either party. Disclosure may not take place between any party external of the contract such as the public. In addition, the recipient agrees no duplication, distribution, or the permission to external parties to duplicate or distribute any related material currently available.

Brown Investment Group (DBA Lavish Wash) agrees fully with written and verbal consent.

Brown Investment Group (DBA Lavish Wash) retains all title, ownership, and intellectual property rights to the material and trademarks presented within this document and related written, verbal, graphic, internet-based, or multimedia presentation thereof.

BY ACCEPTANCE OF THIS DOCUMENT, THE RECIPIENT AGREES TO BE BOUND BY THR AFOREMENTIONED STATEMENT.

Executive Summary

Brown Investment Group (DBA Lavish Wash) is confident and pleased to present All-City Public Schools with this proposal entitled, "The Lavish Bus Wash Endeavor" project. We are aware that considerable thought goes into budgeting in these challenging economic times, specifically when it comes to maintenance and function of transportation. The maintenance and detailing of bus fleet cleanliness is a high priority All-City Public Schools engages in throughout the school year. We are aware of the special and unique opportunity to provide All-City Public Schools high-quality, low-cost cleaning services for the APS bus fleet. Brown Investment Group (DBA Lavish Wash) knows that providing such cleaning services at a significant price is inviting. In the cleaning and detailing services market, often individuals appear to take advantage of companies and others unaware of pricing relative to the service they receive. We-- at Brown Investment Group (DBA Lavish Wash) -- provide consistent, quality service above market standards to ensure our customer's satisfaction in order for business to continue for years.

After reviewing the number of components in All-City Public Schools bus fleet's current situation, Brown Investment Group (DBA Lavish Wash) knows we can serve APS' needs. Our objective is to establish a bus cleaning schedule that satisfies a key quota of buses cleaned per week for a reasonable price. This will be practical and satisfying for both parties during the 2011-2012 year. We will wash each bus for the total cost of $35, considering a fleet of 330 trucks transferring 30,000, twice a day. In order to retain All-City Public schools' business we will:

- Will provide an initial, complimentary bus cleaning demonstration (one bus) to exhibit our technique, precision, and time-management skills.
- As stated, wash each bus for $35, the cost of washing and detailing a midsize sedan.
- Save the APS school bus fleet money usually allocated for cleaning the transportation by providing water, gas, electricity, chemicals, and supplies.
- Reinvest 10% of the revenue received from APS into the school system.

Brown Investment Group (DBA Lavish Wash) possesses a number of dynamic and amazing skills in the automobile washing and detailing service and our experience in this field is paramount. We have experience cleaning cars and tour buses. We will make a reputable partner in this endeavor. We are pleased to engage in such a service endeavor with All-City Public Schools.

Company Information

Founded in 1998 by Daryl Brown (http://www.LavishwashAll-City.com/), Brown Investment Group (DBA Lavish Wash), located in Smyrna, GA, has been essential to the metropolitan area. Brown Investment Group (DBA Lavish Wash) has had various endeavors with a great deal of corporation accounts for over 5 years to date. These clients are still benefitting from our service currently. Even though unemployment is rampant throughout the entire country, Brown Investment Group (DBA Lavish Wash) has been financially enabling individuals via creating jobs. The ultimate goal is to return a 10% of the revenue we receive from APS and reinvest those funds into the APS system, specifically for students.

With 30,000 students being transferred twice-daily in 330 buses, Brown Investment Group (DBA Lavish Wash) is a name synonymous with success and efficiency.

Mission Statement:

We will provide quality auto cleaning service with every client on every occasion. Whether at out facility or at a client location, the client will have a pleasant experience and a pristine looking automobile.

Services Provided

- Mobile Hand Car Detailing
- Hand Car Washing Services
- Car Shampoo
- Car Waxing
- Car Wash
- Car Detail
- Hypoallergenic Cleaning (killing infectious disease, germs, or bacteria)

Offices Location

3485 N. Hill St.SE
 Smyrna, Georgia 30080
(770) 972-0786
info@lavishwashAll-City.com

Identification of Needs

- Thorough cleaning of bus fleet on a regular basis.

- Seasonal detailing of vehicles.
- Providing cleaning services for vehicle in conjunction with special events.
- Cleaning with non-toxic, water soluble, industrial-strength liquid soap for the use of auto cleaning.
- Disposing of liquid waste in an OSHA-regulated fashion.
- Establishing and maintaining clear and concise financial and legal documentation.
- Maintaining a transparent and professional relationship.

Project Scope

- This project involves the staff of Brown Investment Group (DBA Lavish Wash) cleaning and detailing the bus fleet of 330 vehicles over the course of 180 days (the 2011-2012 school year).
- Implementing this plan of action will significantly improve surpluses generated from subsidies acquired by state and federal institutions, thus saving APS money.

The Reason Why Brown Investment Group (DBA Lavish Wash) Is the Best Choice

- Benefits of the proposed plan will save APS a significant amount of money quarterly
- Provide a third party for this task, allowing for APS bus fleet staff to focus on other endeavors
- On specific occasions, Brown Investment Group (DBA Lavish Wash) will provide job assignments for temporary workers in conjunction with cleaning services for APS.

Implementation Plan

Cost Breakdown and Required Work Hours

- At $35 a bus (in circulation), $46,200 would be spent per month, at $277,200 spend per 180-day school year.
- Considering 330 buses being cleaned twice a week with the average of 50 work days.
- 6 to 7 buses would be cleaned a day, with an average bus cleaned or in the process of being cleaned per hour.

Competitive Advantage

- Brown Investment Group (DBA Lavish Wash) has over 13 years of experience.
- 5 years of significant corporate contract experience.
- Numerous rewarding experiences in commercial auto cleaning.
- Brown Investment Group (DBA Lavish Wash) has been a well-known brand in Smyrna, GA and throughout Cobb County for years.
- We use state-of-the-art water containment units, soap dispensers, and a variety of cloths and towels that are lint-free, leaving a more pristine shine following waxing.
- Customer service that is flexible, knowledgeable, and dedicated to exceeding customer goals and expectations.

Payment Terms

- All production, service, man-hours, travel expenses, and or general costs external of materials will be billed to All-City Public Schools. Total costs are subject to approval of the number of buses cleaned. The proposed price by Brown Investment Group (DBA Lavish Wash) is $35 per bus.

- Payments shall be made 30 days after receipt of invoice. There is no start-up fee or deposit required. Late payments will require an additional 50% cost of per bus cleaned. This additional cost will be added to the overall balance on the first day following the original agreed date of payment.

- Payment must be remitted via certified check or electronic payment means provided by All-City Public Schools.

Guarantees

- Brown Investment Group (DBA Lavish Wash) will provide the following offers:

- Bus cleaning of all vehicles in-service will take place one day after the beginning of each quarter.

- If for any reason Brown Investment Group (DBA Lavish Wash) exceeds the total cost, it will be subject to a penalty of 10% of the exceeded amount.

- Brown Investment Group (DBA Lavish Wash) will adhere to the laws and standards of All-City Public Schools, OSHA, and the state of Georgia.

Conclusion

Brown Investment Group (DBA Lavish Wash) is confident that our proposed cleaning strategy for your bus fleet will save All-City Public Schools money and provide them with quality cleaning. In addition, it will provide them time to focus on other endeavors and allocate the surplus generated from savings into other projects and ventures. We are happy and hopeful that APS will be more than pleased to enter a beneficial partnership in this bus cleaning endeavor over an extensive amount of time. We are always available to address comments, questions, and concerns that All-City Public Schools may possess. We look forward to discussing such options in further detail.

Following the review of this document in order to establish a final agreement, please provide the following:

- Submission of questions/suggestions
- Counter proposal or approval by All-City Public Schools
- Negotiation of fees, terms, citations, and conditions

We declare the offer to be binding and free of errors or omissions. Via the diligent and professional performance of ensuring compliance with APS requirements and service needs, we agree to hold our proposal open until August 31, 2011.

Thank you for your interest and time.

Sincerely,

Daryl Brown
Owner/Operator
Brown Investment Group (DBA Lavish Wash)

Chapter VI: The Non-Profit Business Plan

A non-profit bottled water company, seeking to refresh and hydrate the world.
Website: www.goodwater.com

Good Water
Address: 123 AnyStreet Rd.
City and State: All City, GA 30123
(404)/321-1234
goodwater@gmail.com

CONFIDENTIALITY AGREEMENT

This agreement is to acknowledge that the information provided by Good Water in this business plan is unique to this business and confidential. No parties reviewing this information may disclose the contents of this business plan without written consent by Good Water. Any violations of this agreement can result in litigation against such parties that commit this action including other related punitive measures due to such aforementioned actions and/or related violations of confidentiality.

Upon request, this document is to be immediately returned to Good Water, Inc.

Signature _____

Name [typed or printed] _____

Date _____

This is a business plan for Good Water. The presentation of this business plan does not imply an offering of securities.

Master Outline

1.0 Executive Summary
1.1 Objectives
1.2 Mission Statement
1.3 Keys to Success
2.0 Company Summary & Ownership
2.1 Company History & Location
2.2 Start-up Summary
2.3 Start-Up Requirements
3.0 Service Description: The Programs & Implementation Strategy
3.1 Comparable Companies & Competitive Edge
3.2 Sourcing, Fulfillment, & Technology
4.0 Market Analysis Summary, Market Segmentation, and Needs
4.1 Market Trends, Analysis, & Growth
4.2 Marketing & Promotions Strategies
5.0 Strategic Alliances: Partnerships
6.0 Organizational Structure
6.1 Administration, Management & Staff upon Program Expansion
6.2 Employee Requirements
6.3 Adherence & Compliance, Elections, and Promotions
7.0 Financial Plan

7.1 Expenditure Explanation
7.2 Fund Raising Endeavors
7.3 Important Assumptions
7.4 Projected Surplus within Seven Years
7.5 Future Services & Long-term Plan
    Explanation
8.0 Summary
8.4 References

Executive Summary

Good Water is a proactive non-profit organization that advocates numerous programs of enriching empowerment for client populations consisting of disadvantaged, displaced, and disenfranchised individuals. Good Water promotes self-sufficiency and independence among individuals who have for years been considered fringe populations that are marginalized due to social stratification. Good Water exemplifies social change with the intention to inspire, instruct, and inform client populations in means of how they are an integral part of their given communities and will provide steadfast support and assertive action to fortify an all-incorporating foundation of progress and prosperity.

Requested Funds for Good Water Endeavors

For decades, tax payer costs continue to rise when considering the funding needed to support populations that are offenders in transition or ex-offenders seeking stability, school-aged children and teens, and assisting the unemployed and underemployed. This is why the Good Water Endeavors are essential. These endeavors (programs) will provide assistance for the selected client populations and financial relief for taxpayers.

Minnie Fresh is the founder, owner, and operator of Good Water. As a leader in the community and instructor in numerous areas of life coaching and human services, Minnie Fresh is aware of the need for funding to be afforded to Good Water. All spending will be accounted for, and the returns achieved will exceed government subsidies awarded.

The proposed amount of start-up funding to initiate this endeavor is $65,000. The financial projections [section 2.3 Start-Up Summary] illustrate monthly/annual expenditures and annual revenues. With this in mind, Good Water will be able to assist in the needed development among the client populations it serves and establish new means of networking and resource exchange among numerous individuals and entities within communities throughout All City, GA, the state of Georgia, and the United States.

1.1 Objectives

- The purpose of the Good Water Endeavors is to serve as a compound or umbrella program.
- Advocating and assisting displaced, disenfranchised populations via human services, life coaching, empowerment, and enrichment.
- Assistance will be served primarily throughout All City, GA, secondly throughout the Southeast, and thirdly throughout the United States.
- The unemployed and underemployed, adult, client populations will be educated and empowered in order to convert from individuals with challenged personal and professional instances into individuals who are self-sufficient, have an overall positive sense of well-being, and possess expendable income via substantial employment for the private sector and taxable income for the public sector.

1.2 Mission Statement

Good Water is founded on the continuous campaign to inform, instruct, and inspire populations that currently contend with a number of sociological, educational, and socioeconomic challenges which affect such individuals adversely. Good Water's purpose is not only to expand the conventional parameters of life, the necessities in the modern world for survival, but to enrich client populations in order for them to thrive beyond the historic limits often associated with such individuals that are being served by human service organizations. Once stable, the same client populations will invest in others who are currently disadvantaged, thus continuing the cycle of growth and success.

1.3 Keys to Success

As a human services organization, rooted primarily in life coaching, addressing the development of client populations' combined potential is the priority of Good Water. Life coaching assists people in self-epiphany, accessibility to needed resources, and discovery of new and applicable skills that enhance the evolution of such individuals into attaining and maintaining the betterment of their lives. Once this evolution has taken place, supported via the essential resources, then client populations can attain the level of education, careers, residency, and involvement they seek, thus changing the dynamic of success within their given community.

Good Water is established as a non-profit organization [501(c)3 pending status]. The ownership is under the administration of Founder, Owner, and Operator, Minnie Fresh. Any questions or comments concerning Good Water can be directed to Minnie Fresh.

2.1 Company History& Location

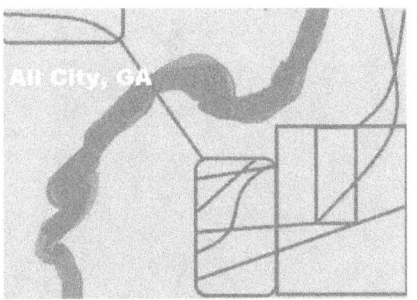

Good Water was established in 2009, located at 123 AnyStreet Rd, All City, GA 30123. The primary reason for Good Water was to assist disadvantaged individuals in investing time and energy in order to improve themselves and establish a more competitive edge. The competitive edge would address points of improvement in general education, community, and the career environment with a sense of personal edification and happiness in mind.

2.2 Start-up Summary

Good Water's start-up expenses come to a total of $65,000. This amount covers the initial location's rent, utilities, print and online media (i.e. pamphlets and SEO endeavors), salary for staff, shuttle service for client populations, business software, computers, signage, furnishings (i.e. tables and chairs) populations. In addition, funding is needed to finance specific operations.

2.3 Start-Up Requirements

Start-Up Assets $0

Start-Up Funding $65,000

Start-Up Expenses

Business Software $1,200

Computers $2,500

Signage	$1,000
Furnishings	$3,000
Overhead Projector/ DVD Player	$910
Movie screen	$139
Basic Textbooks	$1,000
Shuttle Bus	$15,000
Total Start-Up Costs	**$ 24,749**

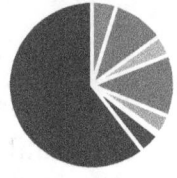

Operating Costs

Fixed Costs per Month

Rent	$5,000
Utilities	$2,000
Professional Staff	$3,000
Maintenance	$1,500
Advertising	$2,000

Movies	$20
Concessions (Events)	$275
Client Stipends	$1,250
Talented Ten Lodging	$500
Book Club Award	$10.41
(per year	$125)
Legal Services (Retainer)	$716.08
(per year	$8,593)
Total Fixed Costs	
per month	$21,771.50
(per year	$195,258)

Variable Costs per Month

Speakers	$1,000
Gas	$531
Total Variable Costs	
per month	$1,531
(per year	$18,372)

Total Operating Costs

per month	**$16,726.67**

(per year $213,630)

Operating Costs

- Rent
- Utilities
- Staff
- Maintenance
- Advertising
- Movies
- Concessions
- Stipends
- Speakers
- Gas
- Awards
- Legal
- Women's Loging

Forecasted Revenue (Annual)

Fundraising Events

Holiday Events Total $38,050

Good Water Employment Training Endeavors

    Total $120,000

Kids' Events Events Total $13,580

Donations/Subsidies Total $42,000

Total Annual Revenue $213,630

3.0 Service Description: The Programs & Implementation Strategy

[Example]

Client populations will learn and/or receive additional training in trades such as automobile repair and maintenance, construction (residential/commercial/industrial), and manufacturing and assembly. In addition, clients will receive instruction in business management, human resources, office support, retail, sales, and other related professions, including entrepreneurial endeavors. Clients will learn about necessary occupational standards such as compliance and adherence laws according to the Equal Employment Opportunity Commission (EEOC) and Occupational Safety & Health Administration (OSHA). Good Water within the Good Water Employment Training program will work as a liaison with both private and public sector partners (i.e. HUD, the U.S. and state Department of Housing). These partners will provide job training experiences for client populations involved. In addition, community-based partners (i.e. philanthropic groups and foundations) that possess general projects that further provide job training and performance experience will share beneficial reciprocity with the Good Water participants. The cornerstone of the Good Water initiative is to educate unemployed and underemployed clients in reestablishing occupational and economic stability, to excel, and to innovate new means to improve and reinvest in their given communities.

A monthly stipend will be afforded to all those that maintain active status and substantial performance in the Good Water program. If a client leaves, program funding will be cut off, immediately. No call, no show means no reentry into the program. Any form of illegal activities and/or legal conflicts involving pending judgment on the aforementioned violations will lead to a client's removal from the program. However, a more proactive outcome would be if a client does achieve a job position while in the program. It is understood that he or she will have to leave; however, Good Water will be more than pleased to serve as professional reference in the former client's favor. The program will provide a certificate of completion for all clients who achieve the needed benchmark in the imitative. The period of completion will take place within a year with quarterly assessments which will reflect actual aptitude proficiency and general trade skills attainment. Good Water will provide general GED training and college-entry preparation exams that can be applicable once clients seek such achievements.

3.1 Comparable Companies & Competitive Edge

Drip Drip, Inc is set on fortifying the bonds between children and families. Drip Drip, Inc. serves not only metro All City, GA, but throughout the state of Georgia. The organization seeks to maintain unity in a family before children become incorrigible and end up as delinquents or in foster care. Drip Drip, Inc. works directly with the Juvenile Justice System.

3.2 Sourcing, Fulfillment, & Technology

Good Water is more than capable of satisfying all fulfillment requirements. This includes all supplies and equipment involved, whether in use or in an inventory. Fulfillment will never be a high concern due to a capable staff trained with the purpose to maintain a balanced state in correlation of fulfillment requirements. Good Water is in a primary position to be substantially influential based on the technology at hand (i.e. desktops and laptops, fax machines, cell phones and business phones, websites, email, copiers, and scanners).

4.0 Market Analysis Summary, Market Segmentation, and Needs
General Population

All City, GA has a population of 269,000 (2012). The majority of the population resides in metro All City, GA. 69% live in urban areas; 31% live in rural areas. All City, GA is the twentieth largest geographical county in Georgia (1,579 sq. mi. of land and 84.2 sq. mi. of water). Individuals between 5 and 18 years are 18.9% of the population. Individuals between 18 and 65 are 26.8% of the population. Out of the entire 269,000, 37% are male; 63% are female. 47 is the median age. 73.0% are Caucasian, 13.0% are African American; 11.4% are Hispanic/Latino. 84.8% of the total population have a diploma; only 17.1% have a Bachelor's degree or higher. 23% do not own their homes. 17.3% live below the poverty line. 78% of the jobs are in the private sector, 13% of the jobs are in the public sector; 8% are self-employed or from an undocumented source ("State &County QuickFacts"; "All City, GA").

The Workforce and Unemployment

Between 2011 and 2013 unemployment in All City, GA was between 12% and 14.5%. Unemployment rate dropped to 7.5% in All City, GA from 7.8% between April and May 2013 and was 2.1% lower from the May 2012 which was 8.6%. Job growth has increased by 3.2% with 2,900 new jobs as of the 2013 year compared to only 1.6% growth in 2012. Growth was proactive in 2013 and expected to rise in 2014.

4.1 Market Trends, Analysis, & Growth

Market trends have been shaped by the recession and bankruptcies over the last ten years. Hospitals, clinics, counseling institutions, and general job placement service centers have closed or merged.

There is a key trend for non-profits in human services to be far more accountable and compassionate with clients versus in years past where non-profits engaged in generalization, thus overlooking key areas in which to assist client populations far more effectively, especially in human services. There has been a significant rise in mental health and addiction treatments within the last five years primarily funded by the public sector (i.e. Medicaid) versus private sector. There also have been numerous concerns into addressing developments in data and means to assess the legitimacy and effectiveness of treatments, time management, assistance strategies, technology, and direct client-staff communication. (Hemmelgarn, Glisson, & James, 2006, 73-89; "Surviving & Thriving").

4.2 Marketing Strategies

The marketing strategy is rooted primarily in the ability to acquire substantial government subsidies from local, state, and federal entities. As far as the private sector, partnerships will arise from local companies that can provide donations and job training experiences for client populations. Donations will also be gained primarily from soliciting non-partner corporations. Product placement of donating entities and subsidy providers will be established during events, within key sales literature, and web advertisements. In addition, solicitation of donations from the general public will take place at Good Water events, partnering company events, non-partnering corporation events, and solicitation within the public arena.

5.0 Strategic Alliances: Partnerships

Partnerships that Good Water develops with corporations will be long lasting and beneficial to both parties. These corporations and companies will be primarily located within physical distance of Good Water's corporate office in All City, GA, initially. Later, the partnerships will expand as new Good Water offices flourish throughout Georgia, the Southeast, and later the entire United States.

6.0 Organizational Structure

Initially, the administration will be lead solely by Minnie Fresh as Owner and Operator. Following Minnie Fresh, there will be three members of an administrative team who instruct three managers. Later, once Good Water is established, the level of complexity within the organization will demand a larger scale of administration, management, and staff. Initially, all employees will be classified under part-time with 2 to 10 hours of work. All members of staff are required to have a Bachelor's degree with the intention of pursuing a Master's after two years of employment.

6.1 Administration, Management & Staff upon Program Expansion

Here, is the personnel plan following two to five years of Good Water's operation. The personnel plan will be based on the manner and form of any corporation. There will be a basic administration established. The administration will contain a CEO, CFO, and COO. Among these positions, individuals can simultaneously hold the positions of President, Chairperson, or a Director. However, the individuals cannot hold more than two positions at a time; this will reduce conflicts of interests and ensure due process. All executives can witness and attend all board meetings held by the Board of Directors and Chairperson. The Board of Directors will be made up of five individuals that address executive, financial, operational functions, partnership and subsidy development, and publicity-related interests; therefore, there will be an Executive Director, Financial Director, and Operational Director (who work under their chiefs the CEO, CFO, and COO), addressing internal affairs and two Directors of external affairs, addressing funding provisions, the Director of Partnerships and Subsidies, and publicity, image assessment, and community interaction. The Director of Public Affairs. The Board of Directors will primarily deal with any committees formed in respond to interests in secondary development or concern when they arise.

6.2 Employee Requirements

All administrative and management positions will be full-time, all staff positions will be part-time, varying from 5 to 20 hours of work. All potential staff members are required to have a Bachelor's degree previous to employment with the intention of attaining a Master's after two years of employment. All administrators and management are required to have their Master's degree previous to employment.

6.3 Adherence & Compliance, Elections, and Promotions

Good Water will enforce all regulations of the EEOC (Equal Employment Opportunity Commission), FMLA (Family Medical Leave Act), OSHA (Occupational Safety & Health Administration), and ADA (Americans with Disabilities Act, pending clients are physically and mentally capable of completing tasks, proficiently). All administrative elections will take place annually with the exception of unforeseen instances such as death, long-term illness, termination, relinquishment of position (due to attaining a lower position within Good Water or another position elsewhere), or extensive leave of absence from 91 to 180 days. In an employee's absence either his or her subordinate or a unilateral member of administration will assume his or the work endeavor and accountability thereof with a substantial portion of the former member's agreed salary at the time. Assessments will take place every three months. Promotions will take place when needed upon program expansion. Demotions will take place when objectives and goals are not met or there is some form of ethical violation which may result in arbitration and immediate termination if necessary.

7.0 Financial Plan

The overall financial plan of Good Water is simple; it seeks to establish a balanced budget where expenditures are matched by revenues within the financial and operational requirements as a non-profit organization. However, as time progresses and success manifests in revenues higher than expenditures, Good Water will further invest into client populations. These investments will expand funding for current and future services along with developments of the Good Water program per milestone tier as far as statewide, regional, and national expansion.

7.1 Expenditure Explanation

The basic expenditures are self-explanatory as far as rent, utilities, professional staff, maintenance, advertising, movie-related equipment, movies for "Kids Events", the Book Club award, and the legal services (retainer). Those are the primary fixed costs. The variable costs, specifically for the first two years will be speakers and gas; however, this list will grow as Good Water develops and expands its programs. Maintenance includes groundskeeping. Advertising includes all forms of online and print marketing such as banners, links, videos, TV ads, radio ads, posters, pamphlets, and business cards. The total for the first and second year of expenditures is forecasted to be $213,630.

7.2 Fund Raising Endeavors

[Example]

There are eight "training endeavors" or "field activities" in the Good Water Training Endeavors program will generate a needed $240,000 per year. 50% will be retained as revenue for Good Water; the other 50% will be utilized as monthly stipends for Good

Water participating clients. The "training endeavors" are Facilities Maintenance, Groundskeeping, Office Support, Debris Removal, Skilled Labor, General Labor, Loading/Unloading, and Cleaning. Each "training endeavor" will generate $30,000 a year, $2,500 a month or $250 per Good Water client. $2,500 a month will be donated from partnering companies. Good Water will send 10 clients to 8 locations (80 clients) for training and "hands-on" experience with the intention that such partners will consider the Good Water clients for hire after one year in the Good Water program. As previously stated, each of the clients will receive a stipend of $125 a month; Good Water will utilize the remaining $125 per Good Water participant for reallocation into the budget. Both men and women can apply; no form of bias will be performed separating genders per "training endeavor" location, according to EEOC regulation.

Donations/Subsidies will generate a total of $42,000. The total amount will be utilized as revenue to be allocated into the budget the following year. These sources of revenue will come from the Community, the State Government, the Federal Government, and Corporations. The Community entails local businesses not participating in the Good Water program, but those that afford Good Water with funding; this will also include the general public who donates needed funds. Corporations will be designated as state, regional, or national for-profit organizations that provide funds for Good Water, but are not "partnering companies" participating in the Good Water program. The Community will provided $12,000. The State Government will provide $9,000. The Fed Government will provide $6,000. Partners will provide $15,000, annually.

7.3 Important Assumptions

Good Water more than likely will have a significant deficit the first two years of operation, based primarily on the Good Water training endeavors along with the Donations/Subsidies if they fall below fiscal expectation; however, if these key fundraising endeavors yield substantial revenues, the deficit will be significantly low, and with the consideration of unforeseen opportunities for grants and partnerships, such agreeable events will compensate for any initial deficits.

7.4 Projected Surplus within Seven Years

The Projected Surplus will be based on a scale of making 150% ($320,445) more in revenue than the initial annual operating costs (expenditures) by the second calendar year, following reception of Start-Up funding; the average rise in revenue expected is 125% ($267,038). By the fifth year, the revenue should be 450% ($961,335) more than the expenditures; however, considering the incremental rise in inflation, realistically the revenue could be as low as 300% ($640,890); the average rise in revenue expected is 375% ($801,113). Following that year, the amount of revenue should plateau for some time, within the next five years with a gradual increase of 10 to 15% each year or an average of 12.5%. Therefore, within seven years of operation, the revenue will be an estimated 362.5% ($774,408) to 512.5% ($1,094,854), an average of 437.5% ($934,631) more than the expenditure with consideration of gradual inflation.

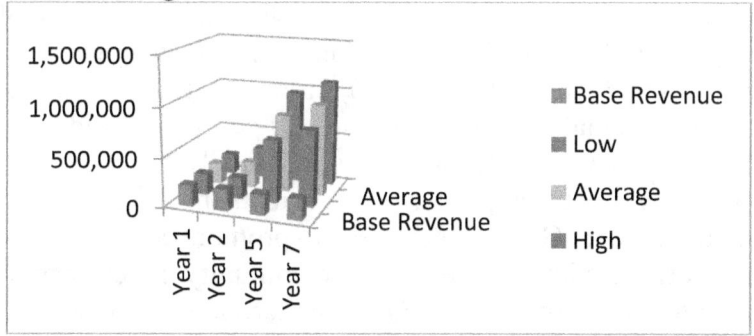

7.5 Future Services & Long-term Plan Explanation

Good Water plans to expand the current services it has and continues to provide. Eventually, a program for former offenders who are fathers of infants will be put in place. There will be more in-depth programs for children and youth of all ages in preparation not only for proficiency testing and exit exams, but exploring and succeeding in areas of creativity in academia, culture, and community. Greater areas of job training will be expanded to include more office-based business management training and training in information technology. In addition, there will be services that address public safety, domestic abuse, and drug addiction in numerous client populations. All of the aforementioned services will be developed and implemented over the next five years within the All City, GA, the Southeast, and later throughout the entire United States.

8.0 Summary

The Good Water will lead in the continuing drive to improve the human condition via human services and social activism, first in All City, GA, second in the Southeast, and third around the U.S.. Good Water will primarily serve men and women, ages 18 to 50, living in urban and metropolitan areas with challenged socioeconomic capabilities that are seeking a GED, currently possess their high school diploma, or seeking/attained degrees yet have become displaced via loss of employment. The purpose of serving the public as a whole is to attend and enable client populations that are disenfranchised, disadvantaged, and displaced to rise above social stratification from self-edification and to fortify themselves socioeconomically, politically, and educationally. Focusing primarily on enrichment and advocacy for client populations, Good Water seeks to promote communication and networking with members of the community in businesses and organizational enterprises. Via Good Water, individuals will experience proactive reciprocity with key individuals and entities within the community and afar that will enable personal growth and achievement to benefit the nation as a whole.

8.4 References

"About" (2014) All City Literacy. Retrieved from
http://www.allcitygaliteracy.org/blog/

Hello, L. (2013, 17 May) "Region's unemployment drops to 7.5%: All City leads Georgia metros

Hemmelgarn, A.L. , Glisson, C., & James, L.R. (2006, Spring). "Organizational Culture and
Climate: Implications for Services and Interventions Research." *Clinical Psychology: Science and Practice.* 13(1), 73–89.

"Surviving & Thriving In This Recession: What Trends Are Shaping the "Recession Marketplace" for Health & Human Services?" (2009) The Open Minds Circle. Retrieved http://www.openminds.com/market-intelligence/intelligence-updates/pebmpioss.htm

"What We Do" (n.d.) Arnette House. Retrieved from
http://dripdrop.org/who-we-are

Chapter VII: The Sponsorship Proposal

Michael J. Hedges
1234 Any Street SE
Vinings, GA 30339
404-707-1447
scriplinque@yahoo.com

November 3, 2013

Sponsor:

Time and time again, single men and women just can't get it together. Love? Romance? Courting? These words seem almost foreign to many today. Dating just doesn't work... or does it?

Hello, I am Michael Hedges, author of the classic book entitled, *Why Dating Doesn't Work!* One of the most popular subjects of today is dating. Why? Well it makes for good reality shows, movies, and books... People are intrigued by the dynamics of males and females constantly trying to figure each other out... and the very nature of attraction and possibility of love touches a universal part of the soul.

Through a number of social network polls, used as feedback, the questions of why dating doesn't work and why it can work were asked. From this, a classic book came into being. At only 70 pages, *Why Dating Doesn't Work!* draws the attention of influential consumers, specifically African American women ages 25 to 50. This book is a conversational piece that draws out questions and reflections in the house, the salon, the spa, even the local clothing store.

When considering all of the brands and businesses that cater to African American women (specifically), there is a massive amount of earning capacity from sponsoring *Why Dating Doesn't Work!* The specific use of the sponsorships will be funding commercials (filming, music, editing, and actors), book signings, webcast/blogcast and radio shows is a lucrative investment. This investment will result in a substantial rise in earnings per month, per quarter, and thus per year. With an average of 5,000 views per week, featuring links and actual products of brands and businesses that sponsor *Why Dating Doesn't Work!* is a significant benefit to add to sponsors' brand recognition and revenue. Here is the link for the premier *Why Dating Doesn't Work!* commercial (launched October 2013) http://www.youtube.com/watch?v=uBthvPMwnOI

Considering that the primary use for your sponsorship at this time will serve as funding for the *Why Dating Doesn't Work!* youtube campaign, my request is a welcomed sponsorship of $50 to $250 per month. The range in amounts is based on four different sponsorship packages. The next series of commercials will be released beginning on Monday, November 25, 2013. All sponsorships will be collected by Sunday, November 24th via invoice online or in-person). Thank you again for your time and interest. A sponsorship proposal will be sent to you at your convenience.

Respectfully Yours,
Michael Hedges

Executive Summary

This proposal contains an explanation of the book *Why Dating Doesn't Work!* and how your brand will be well-represented commercially once your welcomed sponsorship is received. The purpose of *Why Dating Doesn't Work!* is to educate, entertain, and intrigue readers to tap into introspection and assess their strengths and weaknesses in dating and whether or not they are on the right track to having a fulfilling relationship or are in fact ready for one.

Why Dating Doesn't Work! is like a Vidalia onion: sweet 'n' spicy- layered with flavor.

As a sponsor, your brand will be presented to the public within a choice of advertisement packages, offering exposure of your product and/or service in numerous ways. The fact that your brand possesses items synonymous with the primary target market of *Why Dating Doesn't Work!* – African American women, ages 25-50- means that readers will be more likely to be drawn to your brand based on their draw to the book.

A description of *Why Dating Doesn't Work!* will establish the key reasons why so many readers have connected via the first commercial, resulting in purchases either in person from the author or online via amazon.com. The Estimated Itemized List provides a detailed description of the expenditures incurred per month. Estimated earnings per month will be provided. Sponsorship packages and their related benefits will be fully described in order for brands to select the best package for their marketing needs per commercial in which they are featured. Future developments such as other media endeavors (i.e. web radio, webcast shows, a talk show) will be addressed as well.

General Mission Statement

Why Dating Doesn't Work!'s mission is to provide a guidebook, a conversation piece, and a point of interest for deep discussion. *Why Dating Doesn't Work!* is written for the romantic in everyone. It is not mushy or nostalgic, but more so a clear book of questions and answers as to why we choose the romantic partners we do and what about us we may need to change to attract better more compatible people.

With the amount of interest and activity surrounding *Why Dating Doesn't Work!,* via your sponsorship, your brand will receive even greater exposure to potential consumers which will engender significant sales in addition to sales your brand has successfully maintained for years. *Why Dating Doesn't Work!* will introduce your products and/or services via online sales, point-of-purchase sales, book show/tradeshows, interviews, seminars, motivational speeches, blogshows/webcasts, radio commercials, and television commercials.

The Story behind the Book

I was inspired to write this *Why Dating Doesn't Work!* based on the fact that African Americans for the most part are constantly moving toward no sense of romance or connection. Few marry. Many simply indulge in the social fads and lifestyles that lack real communication, compromise, or collaboration needed for relationships. I came up with this topic based on involvement with different social groups on facebook and the fact that being single gets old.

Looking at my own life, I wanted to better understand mistakes I and others make in selection of partners and maintenance of the relationships we have once we establish them. I was married once and plan to marry again. At the time, I am happily single, but still searching. We all need to embrace uniqueness that makes people who they are and stop dating types of people. We need to date others for what makes them actually attractive – originality- men and women alike. Pop culture tries to put everything and everyone into categories- no different from music, books, movies, etc. People are not limited to their "packaging". The cliché is true, "you can't judge a book by its cover." Dating is important as a stepping stone to the seemingly lost or overlooked art of courting which leads to marriage. So many people thrive on making marriage seem deplorable- a point of confinement and loss of freedom. This misinformation has to stop.

Dating has to be seen as a means to learn who a person is and take them for the good and the bad. People will not stay after an argument, but they will tolerate someone who sexually pleases them. That's like trying to live off junk food because we're too lazy to struggle to make a nutritious homemade meal. If we are seeking a long-term relationship, we have to place priority on learning the person's likes, dislikes, aspirations, passions, and "buttons not to push". We can't learn much about a person if we rush into sex and then try to fall back and understand who this person is and what they are about. The lowest form of interaction is sex. So if all we start out with is sex, then in the back of our minds that's all we ever wanted to begin with. If we want a long-term relationship, time works with us not against us. Time only reveals the truth; therefore, there is no rush. Sex will be best with time- anywhere from three months to six months, yet most people barely wait a month these days. They have never had a date, a few phone calls, and then we wonder why dating just doesn't work out.

Author's Bio

I have been told I am a Renaissance man, but to be honest, I have always felt like most people tend to hold back from pursuing their best in all areas of interest and talent. My credo is rooted in reaching one's potential, always being in a process of constant improvement. My background is in education. Currently, I am still involved in tutoring at the post-secondary level. I have a lucrative trade in professional writing and ghostwriting. I am originally from Cincinnati. I have lived in Atlanta approximately 15 years.

Estimated Monthly Costs and Explanation

- Internet Commercials (three that are up to two minutes in length) and Infomercials (one that is two minutes to ten minutes in length)
    Studio Time (Audio Recordings), Imagery (Videography), Graphic Design
    $800
- Actor/Actress' Income $500

- Youtube, Google Ads, Facebook (SEO/SEM, Email Blasts): $800
- Radio and TV Commercials: $1,000
- Travel (Rental Vehicle and Gas, Train, or Plane): $1,000
- Lodging (Motel/Hotel for one to two nights, two to three weekends): $500
- Meals and Refreshments (this includes meals for clients): $300
- Rental Facilities (meetings, seminars): $500
- Book/Tradeshow Booth Rental (a one to two-day event like book signings): $400
- Hard Copies of *Why Dating Doesn't Work!*: $750 per Tradeshow (300 copies $2.50 each)
- Hard Copies of *Why Dating Doesn't Work!*: $500 for copies sold face-to-face, point-of-purchase sales (200 copies $2.50 each)
- Total Needed per Month: $7,650 ($22,950 per quarter; $91,800 per year)
  *This total will increase as sales rise per month, quarter, and year.

With the needed sponsorship of 7,650 per month, the target number of youtube views will be 100,000 per month. Using the universal rule of sales where 10% of consumers approached will make a purchase, 10,000 readers will purchase *Why Dating Doesn't Work!* every month roughly at $3.00 per book. This is a total of $30,000 in sales per month and $360,000 per year by the end of the first calendar year (2014). The youtube campaign will be the primary campaign to market *Why Dating Doesn't Work!* Other means of marketing will include tradeshows, book signings, radio and television commercials, and face-to-face sale presentations (direct marketing). In addition, seminars will serve as a means to not solely sell books but to have open discussions with relationship/romance coaches, couples groups, media groups, and vendors of romantic novelties, products, and services. Along with sponsorships provided by each brand, each brand will be given the opportunity to send print media and products to be displayed in commercials/informercials, at book signings, and at tradeshows/book shows. Also, in order to be placed on the links panels of commercials and block ad panels, emails and logos must be sent.

Sponsorship Advertisement Packages

Even though the price per package covers brand advertisements specifically within the youtube portion of the marketing campaign, brands receive free exposure in other areas of the *Why Dating Doesn't Work!* general marketing campaign. This includes but is not limited to book shows/tradeshows, author interviews and appearances, book signings, radio and television commercials, and other key forms of advertisement mentioned throughout the proposal.

The majority of sponsors will pay for one month of advertisement which will reserve a placement of their ads and/or products for one commercial that will run for one month. However, there will be two other commercials along with one infomercial that will provide additional marketing opportunities. In other words, brands are encouraged for multiple sponsorship provisions per month in order to gain greater brand exposure. For example, if ABC Lipstick, Inc. pays $200 to be listed in the link panel ads, the block panel ads, to feature its products in the commercial, and also mentioned by name, this is covered in one commercial; one commercial runs for one month. When other commercials are scheduled to air within the same month, ABC Lipstick, Inc. can pay for the same package, in this case, the Diamond Pack again or choose among the other three packages for placing an ad in the next commercial, which again provides a substantial amount of brand exposure (i.e. paying for 2 commercials provides 200% exposure; paying for 3 commercials provides 300% exposure, and so on).

Package	Price per Month/Commercial	Features
The Bronze Pack	$50	Links panel ads
The Sliver Pack	$100	Block panel ads (along with the Bronze Pack feature)
The Gold Pack	$150	Product placement in the commercial (along with the Silver Pack features)
The Diamond Pack	$200	Commercials mentioned by name (along with the Gold Pack features)

Package Main Feature Explanations

The Bronze Pack - Links Panel Ad (LPA) – an LPA is an ad that includes the brand's name and website address written on a solid color panel following the *Why Dating Doesn't Work!* commercial/infomercial.

The Silver Pack - Block Panel Ad (BPA) – a BPA is an ad that includes the brand's name, website, and logo or picture of the business, product, service, or owner (it's the brand's choice as to which to display). BPAs like LPAs follow the *Why Dating Doesn't Work!* commercial/infomercial.

The Gold Pack Ad (GPA) – a GPA is an ad where the brand's actual product or a physical reference to the brand's service is represented in a *Why Dating Doesn't Work!* commercial where viewers can see it. Note the actress interacting with the product below:

The Diamond Pack Ad (DPA) – a DPA is an ad where a product or service placed in a *Why Dating Doesn't Work!* commercial is mentioned by name by one or more actors. This may include interacting with the product as in usage or even being on location (i.e. a restaurant may be the product) in some instances. Note the actress referring to the product by name below:

Future Aspirations for *Why Dating Doesn't Work!*

Why Dating Doesn't Work! has already caught the attention of over 15,000 viewers in less than a month and is on the rise. The premier commercial has met great promotional success. Sales from different means of marketing have come to pass, and it is expected that with the holiday season beginning, thousands of sales will take place before the New Year. However, success of a good title is measured by longevity, not immediate sales. Therefore, there must be considerations of future aspirations in the development of *Why Dating Doesn't Work!* as a popular title that will become a classic title.

The future developments for the *Why Dating Doesn't Work!* title and marketing campaign include: more frequent radio and television commercials, the promotion of related titles by the author, a blog show/webcast, and later an Atlanta-based late night television show. The "shows" will be formatted as talk shows. The blog show/webcast will be based on callers, similar to radio shows. The late night talk show will be centered around popular up-to-date trends in romance, dating, marriage, nutrition, health, comedy, news, fashion, sports, consumer trends, entertainment and celebrity personalities (specifically up-and-coming artists, writers, and actors with some established entertainers). Within two years (2016), following the release of *Why Dating Doesn't Work!*, the title will of course be well-known and financially lucrative. The talk show will be regional. Within the following two years after that point (2018), the show will be nationally syndicated.

Summary

Your welcomed sponsorship will benefit both the sales of *Why Dating Doesn't Work!* while extending the your brand among waves of informed, trend-following consumers. *Why Dating Doesn't Work!* is a powerful, no-holds-barred address of the issues that impede romance for a number of people. At the end of the day, everyone wants to be wanted, cherished, respected, and loved. The journey can be difficult, but ignorance makes it harder. Similar to business, romance demands communication, compromise, and collaboration. In respects to brands that sponsor *Why Dating Doesn't Work!* these three aspects hold true and will be mutually beneficial for both my title and your business. Thank you for your interest and investment.

The Book of Business Plans and Proposals: Samples for Your Review

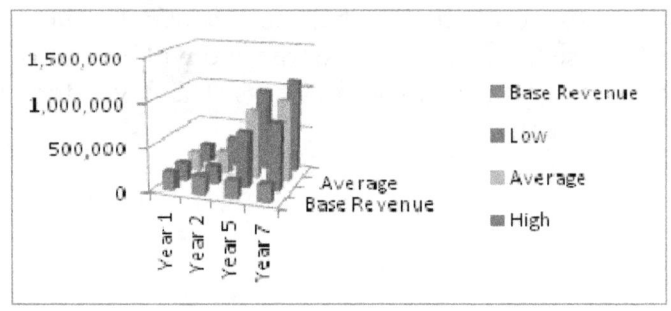

Michael Hedges

www.ingramcontent.com/pod-product-compliance
Lightning Source LLC
Chambersburg PA
CBHW051721170526
45167CB00002B/744